2020 - 2021

by ARGO BROTHERS

1st GRADE COMMON CORE ELA

ENGLISH LANGUAGE ARTS

DAILY PRACTICE BOOK

ARGOPREP.COM

FREE ONLINE SYSTEM WITH VIDEO EXPLANATIONS

ArgoPrep is one of the leading providers of supplemental educational products and services. We offer affordable and effective test prep solutions to educators, parents and students. Learning should be fun and easy! For that reason, most of our workbooks come with detailed video answer explanations taught by one of our fabulous instructors.

Our goal is to make your life easier, so let us know how we can help you by e-mailing us at: info@argoprep.com.

ISBN: 978-1946755421
Published by Argo Brothers, Inc.

Aknowlegments:
Icons made by Freepik, Creaticca Creative Agency, Pixel perfect, Pixel Buddha, Smashicons, Twitter, Good Ware, Smalllikeart, Nikita Golubev, monkik, DinosoftLabs, Icon Pond from www.flaticon.com

BACK to SCHOOL

ArgoPrep is a recipient of the prestigious Mom's Choice Award. ArgoPrep also received the 2019 Seal of Approval from Homeschool.com for our award-winning workbooks.

Want an amazing offer from ArgoPrep?

7 DAY ACCESS

to our online premium content at **www.argoprep.com**

Online premium content includes practice quizzes and drills with video explanations and an automatic grading system.

Chat with us live at **www.argoprep.com** for this exclusive offer.

OTHER BOOKS BY ARGOPREP

Here are some other test prep workbooks by ArgoPrep you may be interested in. All of our workbooks come equipped with detailed video explanations to make your learning experience a breeze! Visit us at **www.argoprep.com**

COMMON CORE MATH SERIES

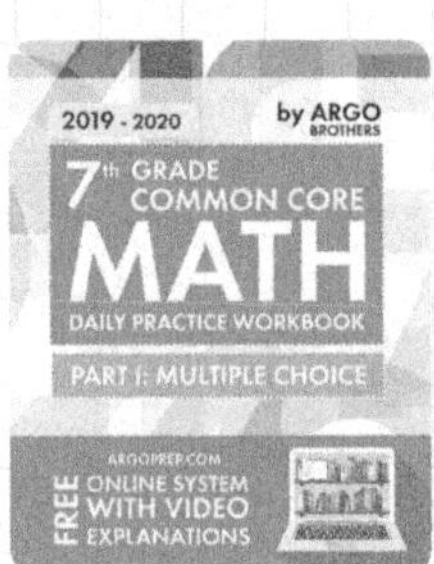

COMMON CORE ELA SERIES

INTRODUCING MATH!

Introducing Math! by ArgoPrep is an award-winning series created by certified teachers to provide students with high-quality practice problems. Our workbooks include topic overviews with instruction, practice questions, answer explanations along with digital access to video explanations. Practice in confidence - with ArgoPrep!

YOGA MINDFULNESS FOR KIDS

HIGHER LEVEL EXAMS

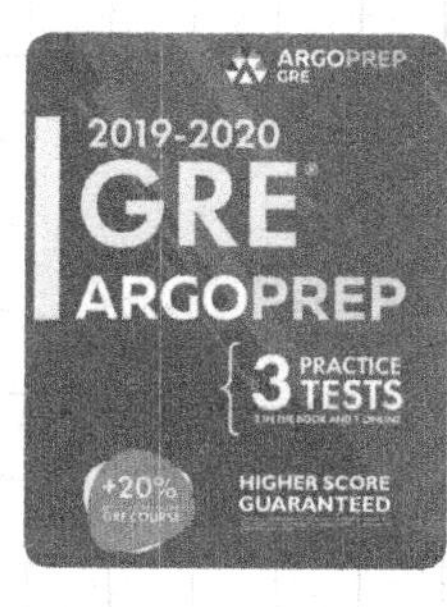

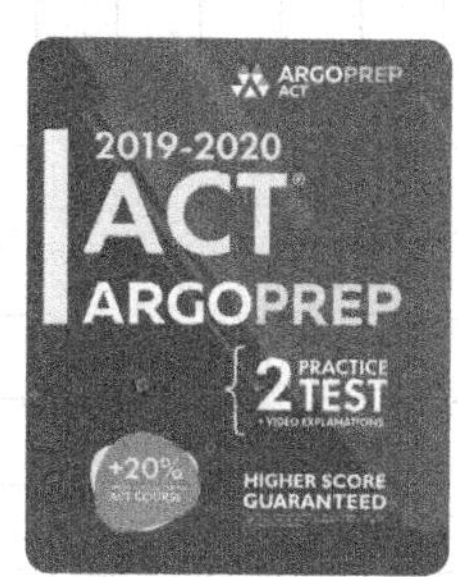

KIDS SUMMER ACADEMY SERIES

ArgoPrep's **Kids Summer Academy** series helps prevent summer learning loss and gets students ready for their new school year by reinforcing core foundations in math, english and science. Our workbooks also introduce new concepts so students can get a head start and be on top of their game for the new school year!

Meet the ArgoPrep heroes.

Are you ready to go on an incredible adventure and complete your journey with them to become a **SUPER** student?

GREEN POISON

RAPID NINJA

CAPTAIN ARGO

THUNDER WARRIOR

ADRASTOS THE SUPER WARRIOR

Our **Kids Summer Academy** series by **ArgoPrep** is designed to keep students engaged with fun graphics and activities. Our curriculum is aligned with state standards to help your child prepare for their new school year.

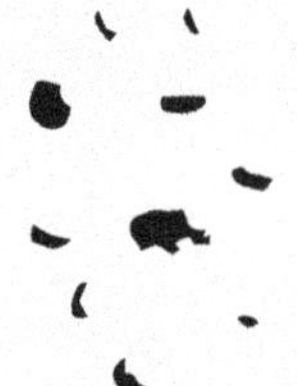

TABLE OF CONTENTS

HOW TO USE THE BOOK

This workbook is designed to give lots of practice with the English Common Core State Standards (CCSS). By practicing and mastering this entire workbook, your child will become very familiar and comfortable with the ELA state exam. If you are a teacher using this workbook for your student's, you will notice each question is labeled with the specific standard so you can easily assign your students problems in the workbook. This workbook takes the CCSS and divides them up among 20 weeks. By working on these problems on a daily basis, students will be able to (1) find any deficiencies in their understanding and/or practice of english and (2) have small successes each day that will build proficiency and confidence in their abilities.

You can find detailed video explanations to each problem in the book by visiting:
www.argoprep.com

We strongly recommend watching the videos as it will reinforce the fundamental concepts.

HOW TO WATCH VIDEO EXPLANATIONS

IT IS ABSOLUTELY FREE

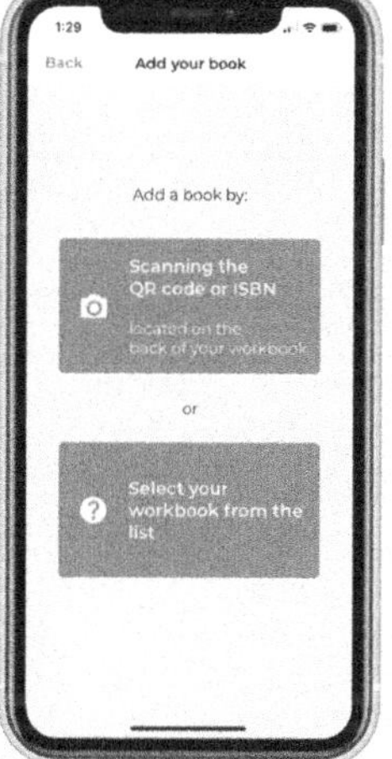

Download our app:
ArgoPrep Video Explanations
to access videos on any mobile device or tablet.

OR

Step 1 - Visit our website at: www.argoprep.com/k8
Step 2 - Click on "JOIN FOR FREE" button located on the top right corner.
Step 3 - Choose the grade level workbook you have.
Step 4 - Sign up as a Learner, Parent or a Teacher.
Step 5 - Register using your email or social networks.
Step 6 - From your dashboard cick on "FREE WORKBOOKS EXPLANATION" on the left and choose the workbook you have.

Lets Begin!

WEEK 1

VIDEO
EXPLANATIONS

ARGOPREP.COM

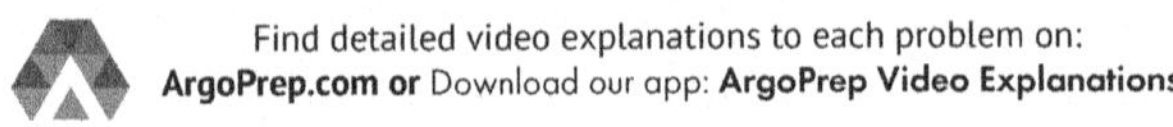

The Lion and the Mouse

Once when a Lion was asleep a little Mouse began running up and down upon him; this soon wakened the Lion, who placed his huge paw upon him, and opened his big jaws to swallow him.

"Pardon, O King," cried the little Mouse: "forgive me this time, I shall never forget it: who knows but what I may be able to do you a turn some of these days?"

The Lion was so tickled at the idea of the Mouse being able to help him, that he lifted up his paw and let him go.

Some time after the Lion was caught in a trap, and the hunters who desired to carry him alive to the King, tied him to a tree while they went in search of a wagon to carry him on.

Just then the little Mouse happened to pass by, and seeing the sad plight in which the Lion was, went up to him and soon gnawed away the ropes that bound the King of the Beasts.

"Was I not right?" said the little Mouse.

Little friends may prove great friends.

Visualize the characters in your head as you read.

Exercises

1. What does the Lion want to do to the Mouse?

   A. He wants to become friends with him.
   B. He wants to chase him.
   C. He wants to eat him.
   D. He wants to tell him a story.

CCSS.ELA-LITERACY.RL.1.1

2. Which word describes the Mouse in the story?

   A. smart
   B. sad
   C. angry
   D. funny

CCSS.ELA-LITERACY.RL.1.3

3. The "King of Beasts" describes:

   A. the Mouse
   B. the Lion
   C. a hunter
   D. a royal King

CCSS.ELA-LITERACY.RL.1.4

4. What happened to the Lion in the story?

   A. He hurt his paw.
   B. He was trapped in a rope.
   C. He did not have any food to eat.
   D. He was sad because he was lonely.

CCSS.ELA-LITERACY.RL.1.3

5. How did the Mouse help the Lion?

   A. He found food for him.
   B. He bit through the rope.
   C. He fixed his paw.
   D. He helped him hide from the hunter.

CCSS.ELA-LITERACY.RL.1.7

6. What lesson can you learn from this story?

   A. It is never a good idea to lie.
   B. Hard work pays off.
   C. Little friends can be great friends.
   D. Anyone can hide from danger.

CCSS.ELA-LITERACY.RL.1.2

The Tortoise and the Hare

The Hare was once boasting of his speed before the other animals. "I have never yet been beaten," said he, "when I put forth my full speed. I challenge any one here to race with me."

The Tortoise said quietly, "I accept your challenge."

"That is a good joke," said the Hare; "I could dance round you all the way."

"Keep your boasting till you've beaten," answered the Tortoise. "Shall we race?"

So a course was fixed and a start was made. The Hare darted almost out of sight at once, but soon stopped and, to show his contempt for the Tortoise, lay down to have a nap.

The Tortoise plodded on and plodded on, and when the Hare awoke from his nap, he saw the Tortoise just near the winning-post and could not run up in time to save the race.

Then said the Tortoise: "Plodding wins the race."

What do you think the setting of the story looks like? The setting is an important part of the story and tells you the place and time that it takes place.

Exercises

1. What does the Tortoise decide to do in the story?

   A. He races the Hare.
   B. He takes a nap.
   C. He goes for a walk.
   D. He wants to tell him a story.

CCSS.ELA-LITERACY.RL.1.3

2. Which word means the same as the word "*boasting*" in the story?

   A. crying
   B. bragging
   C. grinning
   D. running

CCSS.ELA-LITERACY.RL.1.4

3. Why did the Hare stop during the race?

   A. He was tired.
   B. He knew he could rest and still win.
   C. He was thirsty.
   D. He hurt his leg.

CCSS.ELA-LITERACY.RL.1.1

4. Why did the Tortoise win the race?

   A. He was very fast.
   B. He was slow, but steady.
   C. He trained before the race.
   D. He ate a good breakfast first.

CCSS.ELA-LITERACY.RL.1.3

5. Why did the Hare lose the race?

   A. He was very slow.
   B. He tripped on a rock.
   C. He got lost on the path.
   D. He stopped to take a nap.

CCSS.ELA-LITERACY.RL.1.3

6. What is the moral of the story?

   A. Being overly confident can help you.
   B. Exercise is important.
   C. Be kind to everyone.
   D. Slow and steady wins the race.

CCSS.ELA-LITERACY.RL.1.2

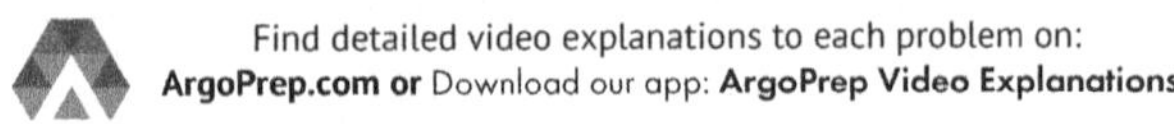

The Ant and the Grasshopper

In a field one summer's day, a Grasshopper was hopping about, chirping and singing to its heart's content. An Ant passed by, bearing along with great toil an ear of corn he was taking to the nest.

"Why not come and chat with me," said the Grasshopper, "instead of toiling and moiling in that way?"

"I am helping to lay up food for the winter," said the Ant, "and recommend you to do the same."

"Why bother about winter?" said the Grasshopper; " we have got plenty of food at present." But the Ant went on its way and continued its toil. When the winter came the Grasshopper had no food and found itself dying of hunger, while it saw the ants distributing every day corn and grain from the stores they had collected in the summer.

Then the Grasshopper knew: It is best to prepare for the days of necessity.

When you come across a word you do not know, read around the word and look for clues from the words that are near it. This can help you to figure out its meaning.

Exercises

1. During what season does the story take place?

   A. Winter
   B. Spring
   C. Summer
   D. Fall

   CCSS.ELA-LITERACY.RL.1.1

2. What does the Grasshopper want the Ant to do with him?

   A. Look for food
   B. Chat with him
   C. Play with him
   D. Sing with him

   CCSS.ELA-LITERACY.RL.1.3

3. Why won't the Ant stop working?

   A. He is bored.
   B. He is building a new home.
   C. He wants food for the winter.
   D. His mother told him to keep working.

   CCSS.ELA-LITERACY.RL.1.4

4. Which word best describes the Ant?

   A. old
   B. kind
   C. tired
   D. hard-working

   CCSS.ELA-LITERACY.RL.1.7

5. What didn't the Grasshopper collect food for winter?

   CCSS.ELA-LITERACY.RL.1.3

6. What lesson can this story teach you? How can you use this lesson to help you?

   CCSS.ELA-LITERACY.RL.1.2

WEEK 2

VIDEO
EXPLANATIONS

ARGOPREP.COM

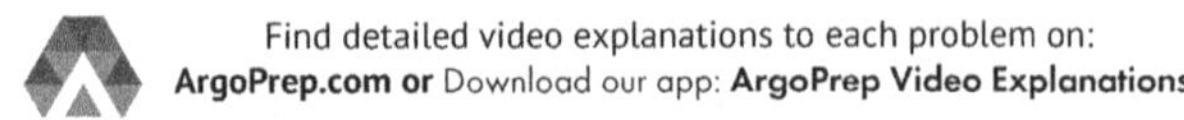

Punctuation

CCSS.ELA-LITERACY.L.1.2.A

How can you share an idea? You share ideas in sentences. **A sentence is a complete thought.** All sentences use **capital letters** and **ending marks.** These ending marks are known as **punctuation marks.**

When you share an idea with someone through speaking, writing, or reading, it is important to show where your complete thought ends.

A sentence ends with a period, a small dot, after the last word. A period looks like this: .

Here are some examples:

We went to the zoo.
We saw many big animals.
We had fun together.

All of these sentences share a complete idea.

Sometimes, we ask questions. **When we ask a question, we use a different ending mark that looks like this: ? and is called a question mark.**

A question mark shows a reader that someone is asking for information.

Here are some examples:

What time is it?
When does your flight leave for your trip?
How long will you be away on vacation?

Someone can respond to these questions with a complete thought that ends with a period. If someone has exciting news to share, his or her thought might end in an exclamation mark instead. **An exclamation mark looks like this: ! and shows a reader to use an excited tone of voice.**

Here are some examples:

I cannot wait for my birthday party!
I had the best day!
We are going to Disney World!

Now, let's practice.

Remember that ALL sentences ALWAYS begin with a capital letter.

Exercises

Choose the complete thought with the correct ending mark.

1. **A.** Where should I go to buy milk.
   B. Where should I go to buy milk?
   C. Where should I go to buy milk!

CCSS.ELA-LITERACY.L.1.2.A

2. **A.** I am meeting my favorite singer in person tonight?
   B. I am meeting my favorite singer in person tonight!
   C. I am meeting my favorite singer in person tonight.

CCSS.ELA-LITERACY.L.1.2.A

3. **A.** Jennifer lives on Mulberry Lane?
   B. Jennifer lives on Mulberry Lane!
   C. Jennifer lives on Mulberry Lane.

CCSS.ELA-LITERACY.L.1.2.A

Read each sentence, and decide which type of ending mark is missing. Write the correct ending mark on the line.

4. What is your favorite food

CCSS.ELA-LITERACY.L.1.2.A

5. I live near Chicago

CCSS.ELA-LITERACY.L.1.2.A

6. I am so excited that my team won the game

CCSS.ELA-LITERACY.L.1.2.A

Capitalization

CCSS.ELA-LITERACY.L.1.2.B

We have learned about using ending marks correctly in sentences. It is important to use capital letters at the right places in a sentence too.

All sentences always begin with a capital letter.

For example:

The dog ran around the tree.

The first word in the sentence starts with a capital letter.

When asking a question, the thought must also begin with a capital letter.

For example:

Will we make it to the movie on time?

The same is true when using an exclamation mark to show excitement in a sentence.

For example:

I cannot believe that we won a trip in the contest!

Let's practice!

Make sure your ending mark can be seen easily when you write sentences.

Exercises

Identify the word that should begin with a capital letter in each sentence.

1. she loves to eat tacos with cheese on them.

A. Tacos
B. She
C. Cheese
D. Them

CCSS.ELA-LITERACY.L.1.2.B

2. they play baseball tonight at seven o'clock.

A. O'clock
B. Baseball
C. They
D. Tonight

CCSS.ELA-LITERACY.L.1.2.B

3. will you go to the park or the mall today?

A. Will
B. Mall
C. Park
D. You

CCSS.ELA-LITERACY.L.1.2.B

4. did she see you near the school?

A. She
B. Did
C. School
D. You

CCSS.ELA-LITERACY.L.1.2.B

5. sam is so excited he doesn't have homework tonight!

A. Tonight
B. So
C. Homework
D. Sam

CCSS.ELA-LITERACY.L.1.2.B

6. the bears walk through that forest.

A. Bears
B. The
C. Through
D. Forest

CCSS.ELA-LITERACY.L.1.2.B

Capitalization

CCSS.ELA-LITERACY.L.1.2.A

Punctuation

CCSS.ELA-LITERACY.L.1.2.B

A complete thought always begins with a capital letter and ends with a period, question mark, or exclamation mark.

Capital letters are used in other places within sentences too.

For example, the word I is always capitalized, like in the sentence:

My mom thinks that I am nervous about the big race.

Here is another example:

She and I love to read books outside in the warm sun.

Names are always capitalized as well. A name identifies a person, and a person is a proper noun. (Proper nouns are always capitalized. We will learn more about proper nouns soon!)

Here are some examples:

The movie was interesting and Mariah liked it.
Ben and Jeff have football practice after school.
The dog loved it when Jessica took him for a walk.

Capital letters and ending marks are both very important parts of sentences.

Let's practice!

Taking the time to include capital letters and ending marks will make your thoughts more clear.

Exercises

1. **Answer the following for questions 1 - 4:**

   Which of these choices is a correct sentence with proper punctuation and capitalization?

   A. Melissa and james live around the corner.
   B. Melissa and James live around the corner?
   C. Melissa and James live around the corner.
   D. Melissa and james live around the corner!

   CCSS.ELA-LITERACY.L.1.2.B

2. **A.** my dad will walk robert to the bus stop!
   B. My dad will walk robert to the bus stop!
   C. My dad will walk Robert to the bus stop?
   D. My dad will walk Robert to the bus stop.

   CCSS.ELA-LITERACY.L.1.2.B

3. **A.** Texas will be a fun place to visit with Sarah.
   B. texas will be a fun place to visit with sarah.
   C. texas will be a fun place to visit with Sarah?
   D. Texas will be a fun place to visit with sarah.

   CCSS.ELA-LITERACY.L.1.2.B

4. **A.** I love to visit the museum on rainy days with john.
   B. I love to visit the museum on rainy days with John!
   C. i love to visit the museum on rainy days with john.
   D. I love to visit the museum on rainy days with John?

   CCSS.ELA-LITERACY.L.1.2.B

5. Write a sentence below that tells about something you like to do. Be sure to use capitalization and the correct ending mark as part of your complete thought.

   CCSS.ELA-LITERACY.L.1.2.B

6. Write a complete thought below that asks about the weather. Be sure to use capitalization and the correct ending mark as part of your question.

   CCSS.ELA-LITERACY.L.1.2.B

WEEK 3

ARGOPREP.COM

VIDEO
EXPLANATIONS

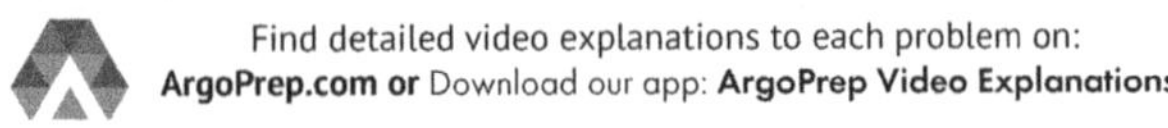

Roller Coaster Ride

Jack ran to the back of the line. He waved at his sister to join him. The summer sun was shining and there were people all over. The smell of popcorn was in the air. Kids were laughing and adults were smiling.

Jack couldn't wait to get on the ride. His sister, Jen, was not so sure. Jen stood nervously near Jack. Jack watched the coaster on the track. Jack watched the people put their hands up in the air. Jen watched too.

Soon, it was their turn. Jack picked the first car in the front. He motioned for his sister to sit by him. They put their seat belts on. The other cars were full, and everyone was ready.

The cars started up the track. They went higher and higher in the sky! The cars made a loud clicking sound. They climbed further and further up in the air. Jack smiled and Jen started to smile too.

Up, up, up they went. The people below looked so small. Jack opened his mouth to scream as the car reached the top. Jen did too, and the car quickly dropped down. Both of them screamed, then laughed. They could feel the speed of the coaster beneath them.

Faster and faster it went as the car turned down another big hill. The two put their hands up in the air. Up up again, and the car climbed back up to the top. Quickly at first, and then slowly it went. The car climbed to the very top, and then it paused.

Jack and Jen waited for it to head down once again. It didn't move, and it didn't go. They could see the amusement park below. They saw tents, games, and other rides. They saw trees, people, and long lines.

After a very long pause, down it went! The rollercoaster twisted and turned again. Jack and Jen screamed and laughed. The ride ended and they got right back in line again.

If you haven't been on a roller coaster yet, you can use clues in the story to help you understand what riding one might be like.

Exercises

1. Where does the story take place?

   A. At the store
   B. At the zoo
   C. At an amusement park
   D. At a museum

   CCSS.ELA-LITERACY.RL.1.1

2. Why does Jen feel nervous?

   A. She cannot find her mom.
   B. She forgot her money at home.
   C. She is lost.
   D. She has never ridden a roller coaster.

   CCSS.ELA-LITERACY.RL.1.3

3. What is the author's purpose for writing the story?

   A. To entertain
   B. To convince you to do something
   C. To teach you about roller coasters
   D. To help you plan a trip to an amusement park

   CCSS.ELA-LITERACY.RL.1.3

4. What happens to the car at the top of the hill?

   A. It gets stuck and they need to be rescued.
   B. It pauses for a long time.
   C. It makes a screeching noise.
   D. It gets rained on when a storm begins.

   CCSS.ELA-LITERACY.RL.1.3

5. Make a prediction. What will Jack and Jen do next?

   A. They will go eat popcorn.
   B. They will go find their parents.
   C. They will ride the rollercoaster again.
   D. They will leave to go home.

   CCSS.ELA-LITERACY.RL.1.4

6. What clue in the story tells you what they will do next?

   A. The smell of popcorn was in the air.
   B. Kids were laughing and adults were smiling.
   C. The ride ended and they got right back in line again.
   D. Jen stood nervously near Jack.

   CCSS.ELA-LITERACY.RL.1.4

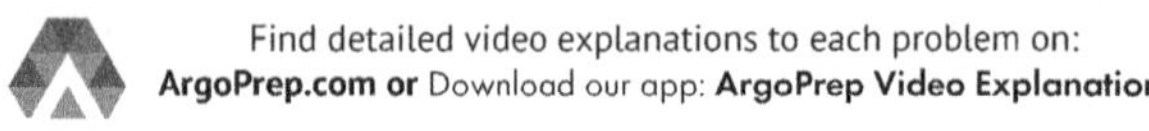

Train Trip

"All Aboard!" the conductor calls. The train's whistle blows loudly and I gather my stuffed animal and blanket on my lap. It's time to leave, and my parents and I are going on a trip to see my grandma.

The doors shut and the train begins to move. I look out the window and watch as it speeds up. Right along the track it goes, slowly at first, and then more quickly. It travels along and passes trees and homes. Soon, the land changes and there are big mountains too.

I notice a boy looking out the window too. He looks sad. An older man is sitting near him and he is holding a stuffed animal too. He looks up at me and smiles slightly. I smile back.

I wonder where he is going. I wonder if he is visiting someone special too. He looks over at me again. My mom tells me that I should try to take a nap because it will be a long ride, so I do.

When I wake up, it is late afternoon.

"Anna, we are almost there," Dad says.

I look over at the boy and he is sleeping too. The train begins to slow down and I can see the station near the track.

The whistle blows again and it comes to a stop. The doors open and we get off of the train. My grandma is there to greet us. She is happy to see us.

As we walk away, I see her wave. I turn to look and see the boy from the train. He waves back at her and smiles. "That's my neighbor's grandson. He is staying here all summer with his grandpa. I'll introduce you to him."

"Okay," I tell her, smiling.

As you read, think about the sounds you might hear while riding a train.

Exercises

1. Where is Anna going?

   A. to see her aunt
   B. to visit her grandma
   C. to school
   D. to church

CCSS.ELA-LITERACY.RL.1.3

2. What does a conductor do?

   A. flies a plane
   B. controls the train
   C. directs traffic
   D. unloads luggage

CCSS.ELA-LITERACY.RL.1.3

3. What does Anna observe about the boy?

   A. He looks sad.
   B. He is tall.
   C. He has dark hair.
   D. He draws nice pictures.

CCSS.ELA-LITERACY.RL.1.1

4. What does Anna do on the train?

   A. She looks out the window and takes a nap.
   B. She reads a book and colors a picture.
   C. She talks to her mom and listens to music.
   D. She eats lunch and reads a book.

CCSS.ELA-LITERACY.RL.1.3

5. Who greets Anna when she gets off of the train?

   A. her aunt
   B. the boy
   C. her grandma
   D. her grandpa

CCSS.ELA-LITERACY.RL.1.3

6. What might happen next?

   A. Anna will get back on the train.
   B. Anna will go to sleep.
   C. Anna will meet the boy from the train.
   D. Anna will go to school.

CCSS.ELA-LITERACY.RL.1.1

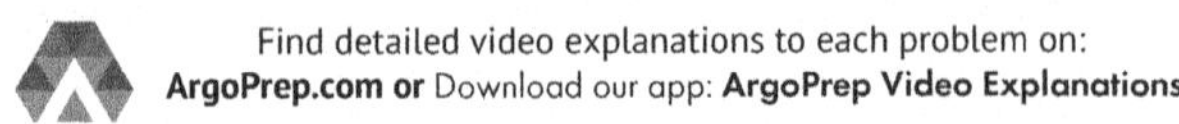

Brittany's Bike

Brittany wanted a new bike. She had a purple bike, but she had gotten taller. It was too small for her.

Brittany's twin brother Brad wanted a skateboard. He was tired of his scooter and all of his friends had skateboards.

Their mom told them that they could ask for a bike and a skateboard for their birthdays. Their birthday was many months away. They did not want to wait that long. They were both impatient.

Brittany's brother had an idea! They would work together so they could get a new bike and a new skateboard. First, they helped their mom around the house. She paid them with money. They put it in an envelope. Next, they helped the neighbors and washed their cars. They tucked that money into the envelope too. Brittany planted flowers while Brad mowed the lawn. Weeks went by and they had walked dogs, held a lemonade stand, painted sheds, and collected trash.

They sat down together to count their money. They smiled at one another when they realized it was time to go to the store.

Their parents took them and they looked around. Brittany picked a new yellow bike. Brad chose a red and black skateboard. They paid for their items at the register.

After their dad put them in the car, Brittany turned to Brad and her parents and said, "We have some money left. Let's go get some ice cream!"

It was nice to enjoy such a sweet treat after all of their hard-work!

Were you able to predict how the story ended? Making predictions as you read can help you to stay on track.

Exercises

1. What is wrong with Brittany's bike?

   A. It has a flat tire.
   B. The handlebar is broken.
   C. The seat fell off.
   D. It is too small.

   CCSS.ELA-LITERACY.RL.1.1

2. What does Brad want to buy?

   A. a skateboard
   B. a scooter
   C. a bike
   D. a football

   CCSS.ELA-LITERACY.RL.1.3

3. What did the kids decide to do?

   A. Work to earn money
   B. Ask for a bike and a skateboard for their birthdays
   C. Wait until the bike and skateboard go on sale
   D. Find something else to do

   CCSS.ELA-LITERACY.RL.1.4

4. Which word best describes the kids?

   A. determined
   B. shy
   C. lazy
   D. kind

   CCSS.ELA-LITERACY.RL.1.7

5. How were Brittany and Brad able to earn money?

   CCSS.ELA-LITERACY.RL.1.3

6. What lesson can this story teach you? How can you use this lesson to help you?

   CCSS.ELA-LITERACY.RL.1.2

WEEK 4

ARGOPREP.COM

VIDEO
EXPLANATIONS

Nouns

CCSS.ELA-LITERACY.L.1.1.B

A noun names a person, place, thing, or idea.

Look at the following sentence:

The tall boy ran by the big tree to get to school.

Which words in the sentence identify a person, place, thing, or idea?

boy

tree

school

A boy is a person.

A tree is a thing.

A school is a place.

Some sentences may only have one noun in them. Other sentences have more than one noun.

Here are some examples:

The cat slept.

My friend likes to play softball.

The boys and their pets play with the ball.

How many nouns are in the first sentence?

There is one noun: cat

A cat is a thing, an animal.

The second and third sentences have more than one noun in each of them.

friend, softball

boys, pets, ball

Nouns can be singular: cat

Nouns can be plural: cats

Singular nouns mean one, while plural nouns means more than one person, place, thing, or idea.

Let's practice!

We need nouns to tell us what the subject of a sentence is.

Exercises

Look at each group of words below. Circle the word that is a noun.

1. **A.** happy
   B. ran
   C. smiled
   D. bunny

CCSS.ELA-LITERACY.L.1.1.B

2. **A.** tall
   B. jewels
   C. jumped
   D. sad

CCSS.ELA-LITERACY.L.1.1.B

3. **A.** car
   B. far
   C. cry
   D. red

CCSS.ELA-LITERACY.L.1.1.B

4. **A.** sing
   B. vacation
   C. look
   D. shiny

CCSS.ELA-LITERACY.L.1.1.B

5. Write a sentence below that tells about a singular place. Circle the noun or nouns you use in the sentence.

CCSS.ELA-LITERACY.L.1.1.B

6. Write a sentence below that tells about a plural thing. Circle the noun or nouns you use.

CCSS.ELA-LITERACY.L.1.1.B

Common and Proper Nouns

CCSS.ELA-LITERACY.L.1.1.B

Nouns name people, places, things, or ideas. Some nouns are very specific. These are known as proper nouns. **Proper nouns begin with a capital letter.**

Some examples of proper nouns are:

Florida

Jennifer

Walmart

Tuesday

Nouns that are not specific are known as common nouns.

Some examples are:

girl

baseball

shoe

store

Look at the following sentence:

Jim and Amanda like to drive their red car in sunny Florida during the summer.

What are the nouns in the sentence?

Jim Amanda car Florida summer

Which of the nouns are proper? Which of the nouns are common?
(Remember that proper nouns begin with a capital letter.)

Proper:	Common:
Jim	car
Amanda	summer
Florida	

Let's practice!

Including proper nouns can help to make your sentence more informative.

Exercises

Identify the proper noun in each sentence.

1. The boys like eating at Burger King.

A. The
B. Burger
C. Burger King
D. boys

CCSS.ELA-LITERACY.L.1.1.B

2. We went to see Jim at his new house.

A. house
B. Jim
C. We
D. new

CCSS.ELA-LITERACY.L.1.1.B

3. In April, the students will go on an exciting field trip.

A. April
B. students
C. field trip
D. On

CCSS.ELA-LITERACY.L.1.1.B

4. What kind of dance class do you take on Wednesday?

A. What
B. kind
C. Wednesday
D. class

CCSS.ELA-LITERACY.L.1.1.B

5. Write a complete sentence and include at least one common noun and one proper noun. Circle the proper noun(s) and underline the common noun(s).

CCSS.ELA-LITERACY.L.1.1.B

6. Write a complete question and include at least one common noun and one proper noun. Circle the proper noun(s) and underline the common noun(s). (Remember to include a question mark!)

CCSS.ELA-LITERACY.L.1.1.B

Possessive Nouns

CCSS.ELA-LITERACY.L.1.1.B

A possessive noun is a noun that shows ownership. This type of noun lets you know that someone has something.

For example, look at the sentence below about the girl's braid:

The girl's braid was long and blonde with a pretty pink bow.

Ask yourself:

What does the girl have?

She has a braid.

Or

Whom does the braid belong to?

It belongs to the girl.

The possessive noun is girl's.

Here is another example:

Josh's cat loves to rest in the kitchen during dinner.

Ask yourself:

What does the Josh have?	Or	Whom does the cat belong to?
He has a cat.		It belongs to Josh.

The possessive noun is Josh's.

(The noun Josh's is also a proper noun too!)

To show possession, we use an apostrophe and the letter s.

Sam's homework	the car's tire	a boy's shoe

When a plural noun shows possession, the apostrophe is located at the end of the word, after the letter s.

siblings' chores	babies' bottles	books' covers

Let's practice!

Using an apostrophe is key when writing a possessive noun. Without it, the noun may look plural instead.

Exercises

Complete each sentence with the correct possessive noun.

1. Mark plays soccer with ________________.

   (the friends of Bill)

   CCSS.ELA-LITERACY.L.1.1.B

2. Tara will listen to the ________________.

   (advice of the doctor)

   CCSS.ELA-LITERACY.L.1.1.B

3. I sorted the laundry and folded my ________.

   (shirts of my brothers)

   CCSS.ELA-LITERACY.L.1.1.B

4. ________________ spilled on the floor.

   (the milk belonging to John)

   CCSS.ELA-LITERACY.L.1.1.B

5. ________________ was soft and warm.

   (the blanket of the baby)

   CCSS.ELA-LITERACY.L.1.1.B

6. ________________ were flat.

   (the tires of the car)

   CCSS.ELA-LITERACY.L.1.1.B

WEEK 5

ARGOPREP.COM

VIDEO
EXPLANATIONS

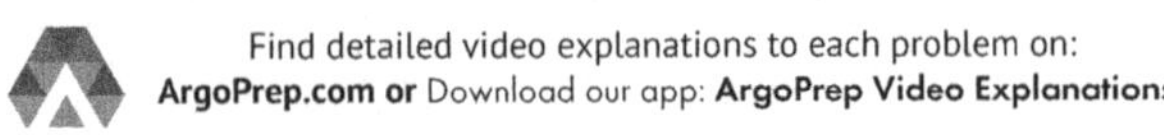

Excerpt from The Tale of Peter Rabbit

Once upon a time there were four little Rabbits, and their names were – Flopsy, Mopsy, Cotton-tail, and Peter. They lived with their Mother in a sand-bank, underneath the root of a very big fir tree.

"Now, my dears," said old Mrs. Rabbit one morning, "you may go into the fields or down the lane, but don't go into Mr. McGregor's garden. Your Father had an accident there; he was put in a pie by Mrs. McGregor."

"Now run along, and don't get into mischief. I am going out."

Then old Mrs. Rabbit took a basket and her umbrella, to the baker's. She bought a loaf of brown bread and five currant buns.

Flopsy, Mopsy, and Cottontail, who were good little bunnies, went down the lane to gather blackberries; but Peter, who was very naughty, ran straight away to Mr. McGregor's garden and squeezed under the gate!

First, he ate some lettuces and some French beans; and then he ate some radishes; and then, feeling rather sick, he went to look for some parsley. But round the end of a cucumber frame, whom should he meet but Mr. McGregor!

Mr. McGregor was on his hands and knees planting out young cabbages, but he jumped up and ran after Peter, waving a rake and calling out, "Stop thief!"

Peter was most dreadfully frightened; he rushed all over the garden, for he had forgotten the way back to the gate.

He lost one of his shoes among the cabbages, and the other shoe amongst the potatoes. After losing them, he ran on four legs and went faster, so that I think he might have got away altogether if he had not unfortunately run into a gooseberry net, and got caught by the large buttons on his jacket. It was a blue jacket with brass buttons, quite new.

Peter gave himself up for lost, and shed big tears; but his sobs were overheard by some friendly sparrows, who flew to him in great excitement, and implored him to exert himself.

Stop after every few paragraphs and ask yourself what happened in what you have read so far.

Exercises

1. Who is the main character in the story?

   A. Peter Rabbit
   B. Mother
   C. Mr. McGregor
   D. Flopsy

CCSS.ELA-LITERACY.RL.1.3

2. Where does the story take place?

   A. In a rabbit hole
   B. In Mr. McGregor's garden
   C. In Mother's kitchen
   D. In the wildflower field

CCSS.ELA-LITERACY.RL.1.3

3. What is the author's purpose for writing the story?

   A. To entertain
   B. To convince you to do something
   C. To teach you about rabbits
   D. To help you understand how to have a rabbit for a pet

CCSS.ELA-LITERACY.RL.1.2

4. What did Mr. McGregor do to Peter?

   A. Gave him some food
   B. Ran after him
   C. Trapped him in a cage
   D. Returned him to his mother

CCSS.ELA-LITERACY.RL.1.3

5. What happened to Peter's jacket?

   A. He left it near Mr. McGregor.
   B. It got caught on a gooseberry net.
   C. He gave it to Mopsy.
   D. It fell into a puddle of water.

CCSS.ELA-LITERACY.RL.1.1

6. What else did Peter lose?

   A. his carrots
   B. his siblings
   C. his way
   D. his shoes

CCSS.ELA-LITERACY.RL.1.3

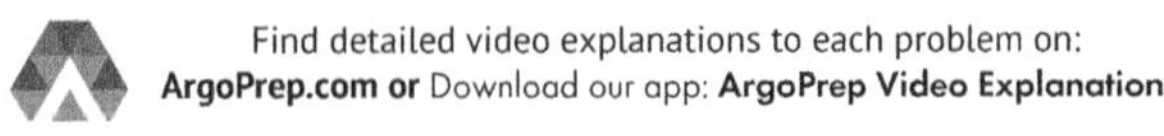

Excerpt from The Tale of Benjamin Bunny

One morning a little rabbit sat on a bank. He pricked his ears and listened to the trit-trot, trit-trot of a pony.

A gig was coming along the road; it was driven by Mr. McGregor, and beside him sat Mrs. McGregor in her best bonnet.

As soon as they had passed, little Benjamin Bunny slid down into the road, and set off--with a hop, skip and a jump--to call upon his relations, who lived in the wood at the back of Mr. McGregor's garden.

That wood was full of rabbit holes; and in the neatest sandiest hole of all, cousins--Flopsy, Mopsy, Cotton-tail, and Peter.

Old Mrs. Rabbit was a widow; she earned her living by knitting rabbit-wool mittens and muffetees (I once bought a pair at a bazaar). She also sold herbs, and rosemary tea, and rabbit-tobacco (which is what we call lavender).

Little Benjamin did not very much want to see his Aunt. He came round the back of the fir-tree, and nearly tumbled upon the top of his Cousin Peter.

Peter was sitting by himself. He looked poorly, and was dressed in a red cotton pocket-handkerchief.

"Peter,"--said little Benjamin, in a whisper--"who has got your clothes?"

Peter replied--"The scarecrow in Mr. McGregor's garden," and described how he had been chased about the garden, and had dropped his shoes and coat.

Little Benjamin sat down beside his cousin, and assured him that Mr.

McGregor had gone out in a gig, and Mrs. McGregor also; and certainly for the day, because she was wearing her best bonnet.

Peter said he hoped that it would rain.

At this point old Mrs. Rabbit's voice was heard inside the rabbit hole, calling: "Cotton-tail! Cotton-tail! Fetch some more camomile!"

Peter said he thought he might feel better if he went for a walk.

Reading stories written by the same author can help you to learn his or her style of writing.

Exercises

1. What did Benjamin Bunny wait for?

   A. He waited for the rain to stop.
   B. He waited for Mr. and Mrs. McGregor to pass by.
   C. He waited for dinner to be ready.
   D. He waited for the sun to come up.

CCSS.ELA-LITERACY.RL.1.1

2. What does the word *relations* refer to in the story?

   A. cousins
   B. widow
   C. siblings
   D. Peter Rabbit

CCSS.ELA-LITERACY.RL.1.3

3. How did Mrs. Rabbit earn money?

   A. She made things by knitting.
   B. She baked pies and sold them.
   C. She cleaned houses.
   D. She baby-sat other small rabbits.

CCSS.ELA-LITERACY.RL.1.3

4. Which item also does the same job as a handkerchief?

   A. a scarf
   B. a mitten
   C. a bib
   D. a tissue

CCSS.ELA-LITERACY.RL.1.4

5. Who has Peter's clothes?

   A. his mother
   B. Mr. McGregor
   C. the scarecrow
   D. Mrs. McGregor

CCSS.ELA-LITERACY.RL.1.3

6. What does Peter decide that he should do?

   A. He will go talk to Mr. McGregor.
   B. He will ask his mother for help.
   C. He will go take a nap.
   D. He will go for a walk.

CCSS.ELA-LITERACY.RL.1.3

Excerpt from The Tale of Squirrel Nutkin

This is a Tale about a tail – a tail that belonged to a little red squirrel, and his name was Nutkin.

He had a brother called Twinkleberry, and a great many cousins: they lived in a wood at the edge of a lake.

In the middle of the lake there is an island covered with trees and nut bushes; and amongst those trees stands a hollow oak-tree, which is the house of an owl who is called Old Brown.

One autumn when the nuts were ripe, and the leaves on the hazel bushes were golden and green – Nutkin and Twinkleberry and all the other little squirrels came out of the wood, and down to the edge of the lake.

They made little rafts out of twigs, and they paddled away over the water to Owl Island to gather nuts.

Each squirrel had a little sack and a large oar, and spread out his tail for a sail.

They also took with them an offering of three fat mice as a present for Old Brown, and put them down upon his doorstep.

Then Twinkleberry and the other little squirrels each made a low bow, and said politely –

"Old Mr. Brown, will you favour us with permission to gather nuts upon your island?"

But Nutkin was excessively impertinent in his manners. He bobbed up and down like a little red cherry, singing –

"Riddle me, riddle me, rot-tot-tote!
A little wee man, in a red red coat!
A staff in his hand, and a stone in his throat;
If you'll tell me this riddle, I'll give you a groat."

Now this riddle is as old as the hills; Mr. Brown paid no attention whatever to Nutkin.

He shut his eyes obstinately and went to sleep.

The squirrels filled their little sacks with nuts, and sailed away home in the evening.

But next morning they all came back again to Owl Island; and Twinkleberry and the others brought a fine fat mole, and laid it on the stone in front of Old Brown's doorway, and said –

"Mr. Brown, will you favor us with your gracious permission to gather some more nuts?"

But Nutkin, who had no respect, began to dance up and down, tickling old Mr. Brown with a nettle and singing –

Try to picture what each character might look like. This can help you to keep track of them as you read.

"Old Mr. B! Riddle-me-ree!
Hitty Pitty within the wall,
Hitty Pitty without the wall;
If you touch Hitty Pitty,
Hitty Pitty will bite you!"

Mr. Brown woke up suddenly and carried the mole into his house.

He shut the door in Nutkin's face. Presently a little thread of blue smoke from a wood fire came up from the top of the tree, and Nutkin peeped through the key-hole and sang –

"A house full, a hole full!
And you cannot gather a bowl-full!"

The squirrels searched for nuts all over the island and filled their little sacks.

But Nutkin gathered oak-apples – yellow and scarlet – and sat upon a beech-stump playing marbles, and watching the door of old Mr. Brown.

On the third day the squirrels got up very early and went fishing; they caught seven fat minnows as a present for Old Brown.

They paddled over the lake and landed under a crooked chestnut tree on Owl Island.

Exercises

1. During what season does the story take place?

   A. Winter
   B. Spring
   C. Summer
   D. Autumn

CCSS.ELA-LITERACY.RL.1.1

2. How did the squirrels get to the island?

   A. They swam.
   B. They walked along the shore.
   C. They floated on rafts.
   D. They flew in a plane.

CCSS.ELA-LITERACY.RL.1.3

3. In the story it says that Nutkin was "excessively impertinent in his manners." What does this mean?

   A. Nutkin was rude.
   B. Nutkin was patient.
   C. Nutkin was kind.
   D. Nutkin was tired.

CCSS.ELA-LITERACY.RL.1.7

4. Besides gathering nuts, what else did the squirrels get?

   A. fish
   B. berries
   C. candy
   D. eggs

CCSS.ELA-LITERACY.RL.1.3

5. How does Mr. Brown feel about Nutkin?

CCSS.ELA-LITERACY.RL.1.2

6. Why did the squirrels bring Mr. Brown three mice?

CCSS.ELA-LITERACY.RL.1.2

Notes

WEEK 6

VIDEO
EXPLANATIONS

ARGOPREP.COM

Verbs

CCSS.ELA-LITERACY.L.1.1.E

You can do many things. You can write, jump, sleep, and laugh. You can run, eat, draw, and sing. These are all action words.

Action words are called verbs. A verb is a word that tells what a person or thing does.

Look at the following sentence:

The baby cries.

Which word in the sentence tells what action is happening?

cries

The word cries tells what the baby is doing.

Look at another example.

Mary and John ate at the restaurant.

Which word in the sentence shows action?

ate

Let's practice!

Verbs are the doing part of a sentence. Without verbs, we wouldn't have sentences.

Exercises

Look at each sentence below. Choose the word that is a verb.

1. Robby sings in the shower.

   A. shower
   B. in
   C. sings
   D. Robby

CCSS.ELA-LITERACY.L.1.1.E

2. The sun shines in the blue sky.

   A. shines
   B. blue
   C. in
   D. sun

CCSS.ELA-LITERACY.L.1.1.E

3. Yesterday, I drove my car to the beach.

   A. Yesterday
   B. my
   C. beach
   D. drove

CCSS.ELA-LITERACY.L.1.1.E

4. In the morning, we eat breakfast together.

   A. breakfast
   B. together
   C. morning
   D. eat

CCSS.ELA-LITERACY.L.1.1.E

5. Write a sentence below that tells about something you can do well. Circle the verb in the sentence.

CCSS.ELA-LITERACY.L.1.1.E

6. Write a sentence below that tells about something you want to do someday. Circle the verb in the sentence.

CCSS.ELA-LITERACY.L.1.1.E

Verb Types

CCSS.ELA-LITERACY.L.1.1.E

All sentences include a subject (someone or something) and a verb. The verb tells what that person or thing does or is. Some verbs show action and some show a state of being.

Action verbs include words such as: run, eat, smile, write, jog, climb.

Linking verbs include words such as: is, are, were, was, am.

Let's look at the difference between these two types.

Mike *laughs* during the funny movie.

Mike *was* at the movies.

In the examples, the verbs are *laugh* and *was*.

Laugh is an action verb. It is something you can do.

Was is an example of a linking verb. It links Mike to being at the movies.

Linking Verbs:

be

being

been

am

is

are

was

were

Let's practice!

Think of the word 'acting' to help you remember what 'action' verbs are. Acting is an action that you can do.

Exercises

Circle the verb in each sentence. Then decide if the verb is an action verb or a linking verb and write it on the line.

1. The stars were bright in the sky.

CCSS.ELA-LITERACY.L.1.1.E

2. We swam in the ocean.

CCSS.ELA-LITERACY.L.1.1.E

3. On Sundays, the family goes shopping.

CCSS.ELA-LITERACY.L.1.1.E

4. We sang during the concert.

CCSS.ELA-LITERACY.L.1.1.E

5. The dog is outside.

CCSS.ELA-LITERACY.L.1.1.E

6. My grandma lives in Florida.

CCSS.ELA-LITERACY.L.1.1.E

Verb Tenses

CCSS.ELA-LITERACY.L.1.1.E

Verbs are action words or words that show a state of being. Different verb endings tell when something happens.

Past tense verbs end in –ed and tell that something has already happened.

Present tense verbs end in –ing and tell that something is happening now.

Future tense verbs that have the helping verb *will* in front tell that something will occur in the future.

Look at the following examples.

Past:	Present:	Future:
walked	walks	will walk
looked	looks	will look
played	plays	will play

Becky laughed at my joke. (past tense)
Becky laughs at my joke. (present tense)
Becky will laugh at my joke. (future tense)

Let's practice!

When you write two or more sentences together, their verb tenses should be the same.

Exercises

Circle the complete verb in the sentence. Decide the correct tense and write it on the line.

1. Megan smiled at the new puppy.

CCSS.ELA-LITERACY.L.1.1.E

4. The storm will bring a lot of rain.

CCSS.ELA-LITERACY.L.1.1.E

2. The teacher talked to the students.

CCSS.ELA-LITERACY.L.1.1.E

5. Her baby cries before his nap.

CCSS.ELA-LITERACY.L.1.1.E

3. I will run the marathon soon.

CCSS.ELA-LITERACY.L.1.1.E

6. We draw in art class.

CCSS.ELA-LITERACY.L.1.1.E

WEEK 7
VIDEO
EXPLANATIONS
ARGOPREP.COM

An Excerpt from The Ugly Duckling

It was beautiful in the country. It was summertime. The wheat was yellow, the oats were green, the hay was stacked up in the green meadows, and the stork paraded about on his long red legs, talking in Egyptian, which language he had learnt from his mother.

The fields and meadows were skirted by thick woods, and a deep lake lay in the midst of the woods. Yes; it was indeed beautiful in the country! The sunshine fell warmly on an old mansion, surrounded by deep canals, and from the walls down to the water's edge there grew large burdock leaves, so high that children could stand upright among them without being seen.

This place was as wild as the thickest part of the wood, and on that account a Duck had chosen to make her nest there. She was sitting on her eggs; but the pleasure she had felt at first was now almost gone, because she had been there so long, and had so few visitors, for the other Ducks preferred swimming on the canals to sitting among the burdock leaves gossiping with her.

At last the eggs cracked one after another, "Chick, chick!" All the eggs were alive, and one little head after another peered forth. "Quack, quack!" said the Duck, and all got up as well as they could. They peeped about from under the green leaves; and as green is good for the eyes, their mother let them look as long as they pleased.

"How large the world is!" said the little ones, for they found their new abode very different from their former narrow one in the eggshells.

"Do you imagine this to be the whole of the world?" said the mother. "It extends far beyond the other side of the garden in the pastor's field; but I have never been there. Are you all here?" And then she got up. "No, not all, for the largest egg is still here. How long will this last? I am so weary of it!" And then she sat down again. "Well, and how are you getting on?" asked an old Duck, who had come to pay her a visit.

"This one egg keeps me so long," said the mother. "It will not break. But you should see the others! They are the prettiest little Ducklings I have seen in all my days. They are all like their father--the good-for-nothing fellow, he has not been to visit me once!"

"Let me see the egg that will not break," said the old Duck. "Depend upon it, it is a turkey's egg. I was cheated in the same way once myself, and I had such trouble with the young ones; for they were afraid of the water, and I could not get them there. I called and scolded, but it was all of no use. But let me see the egg--ah, yes! to be sure, that is a turkey's egg. Leave it, and teach the other little ones to swim."

"What is the matter?" asked the Old Woman.

"I will sit on it a little longer," said the Duck. "I have been sitting so long, that I may as well spend the harvest here."

"It is no business of mine," said the old Duck, and away she waddled.

The great egg burst at last. "Chick! Chick!" said the little one, and out it tumbled--but, oh, how large and ugly it was! The Duck looked at it. "That is a great, strong creature," said she. "None of the others are at all like it. Can it be a young turkey? Well, we shall soon find out. It must go into the water, though I push it in myself."

Use the title of a story as a tool to tell you a little about what you will be reading.

Exercises

1. Where did Duck make her nest?

   A. Close to the school
   B. Near the mansion
   C. By the mountains
   D. Under the bridge

   CCSS.ELA-LITERACY.RL.1.3

2. Where does the story take place?

   A. In the city
   B. In the country
   C. At the beach
   D. Along the river

   CCSS.ELA-LITERACY.RL.1.3

3. What is the author's purpose for writing the story?

   A. To entertain
   B. To convince you to do something
   C. To teach you about ducks
   D. To help you understand how ducks learn to swim

   CCSS.ELA-LITERACY.RL.1.2

4. What did Duck wait a long time for?

   A. The last egg to hatch
   B. The rain to stop
   C. The farmer to go away
   D. The babies to learn to swim

   CCSS.ELA-LITERACY.RL.1.3

5. What kind of egg does the Old Woman talk about?

   A. An ostrich egg
   B. A robin's egg
   C. A goose egg
   D. A turkey egg

   CCSS.ELA-LITERACY.RL.1.1

6. Where is Mother taking the new babies?

   A. To swim
   B. To get food
   C. To make a new nest
   D. To sleep

   CCSS.ELA-LITERACY.RL.1.3

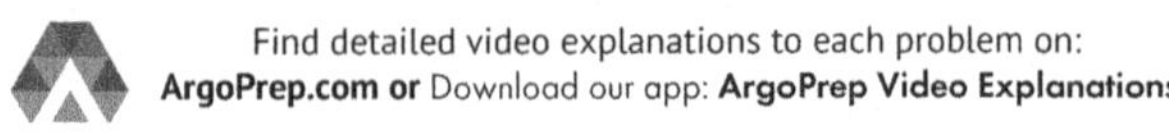

An Excerpt from Aladdin and the Wonderful Lamp

Aladdin was the only son of a poor widow who lived in China; but instead of helping his mother to earn their living, he let her do all the hard work, while he himself only thought of idling and amusement.

One day, as he was playing in the streets, a stranger came up to him, saying that he was his father's brother, and claiming him as his long-lost nephew. Aladdin had never heard that his father had had a brother; but as the stranger gave him money and promised to buy him fine clothes and set him up in business, he was quite ready to believe all that he told him. The man was a magician, who wanted to use Aladdin for his own purposes.

The next day the stranger came again, brought Aladdin a beautiful suit of clothes, gave him many good things to eat, and took him for a long walk, telling him stories all the while to amuse him. After they had walked a long way, they came to a narrow valley, bounded on either side by tall, gloomy-looking mountains. Aladdin was beginning to feel tired, and he did not like the look of this place at all. He wanted to turn back; but the stranger would not let him. He made Aladdin follow him still farther, until at length they reached the place where he intended to carry out his evil design. Then he made Aladdin gather sticks to make a fire, and when they were in a blaze he threw into them some powder, at the same time saying some mystical words, which Aladdin could not understand.

Immediately they were surrounded with a thick cloud of smoke. The earth trembled, and burst open at their feet--disclosing a large flat stone with a brass ring fixed in it.

The word Aladdin might be unfamiliar to you, but you know that it is a type of proper noun because it starts with a capital letter. Aladdin is a character's name.

Exercises

1. Where does Aladdin live?

   A. China
   B. Africa
   C. Egypt
   D. America

   CCSS.ELA-LITERACY.RL.1.1

2. What did the stranger tell him?

   A. He said that he was his brother.
   B. He said that he was his uncle.
   C. He said that he was his father's friend.
   D. He said that Aladdin's mother sent him.

   CCSS.ELA-LITERACY.RL.1.3

3. What did the man bring to Aladdin?

   A. He brought him money.
   B. He brought him toys.
   C. He brought him a new pet.
   D. He brought him clothes.

   CCSS.ELA-LITERACY.RL.1.3

4. What was the stranger's job?

   A. He was a doctor.
   B. He was a musician.
   C. He was a magician.
   D. He was a chef.

   CCSS.ELA-LITERACY.RL.1.4

5. Where did Aladdin go?

   A. on a long walk
   B. to the store
   C. into a castle
   D. to the beach

   CCSS.ELA-LITERACY.RL.1.3

6. How does Aladdin feel after his journey?

   A. He is tired and scared.
   B. He is happy and curious.
   C. He is angry and lonely.
   D. He is excited and proud.

   CCSS.ELA-LITERACY.RL.1.3

Find detailed video explanations to each problem on:
ArgoPrep.com or Download our app: **ArgoPrep Video Explanations**

The Adventures of Tom Thumb

A long time ago, a woodcutter lived with his wife in a small cottage not far from a great forest. They had seven children – all boys; and the youngest was the smallest little fellow ever seen. He was called Tom Thumb. But though he was so small, he was far cleverer than any of his brothers, and he heard a great deal more than anybody ever imagined.

It happened that just at this time there was a famine in the land, and the woodcutter and his wife became so poor that they could no longer give their boys enough to eat. One night – after the boys had gone to bed – the husband sighing deeply, said – "We cannot feed our children any longer, and to see them starve before our eyes is more than I can bear. Tomorrow morning, therefore, we will take them into the forest and leave them in the thickest part of it, so that they will not be able to find their way back."

His wife wept bitterly at the thought of leaving their children to perish in the forest; but she, too, thought it better than to see them die before her eyes. So she consented to her husband's plan.

But all this time Tom Thumb had been awake, and he had overheard all the conversation. He lay awake a long while thinking what to do. Then, slipping quietly out of bed, he ran down to the river and filled his pocket with small white pebbles from the river's brink.

In the morning the parents called the children, and, after giving them a crust of bread, they all set out for the wood. Tom Thumb did not say a word to his brothers of what he had overheard; but, lingering behind, he dropped the pebbles from his pocket one by one, as they walked, so that he should be able to find his way home. When they reached a very thick part of the forest, the father and mother told the children to wait while they went a little farther to cut wood, but as soon as they were out of sight they turned and went home by another way.

When darkness fell, the children began to realize that they were deserted, and they began to cry loudly. Tom Thumb, however, did not cry. "Do not weep, my brothers," he said encouragingly. "Only wait until the moon rises, and we shall soon be able to find our way home."

When at length the moon rose, it shone down upon the white pebbles which Tom Thumb had scattered; and, following this path, the children soon reached their father's house. But at first they were afraid to go in, and waited outside the door to hear what their parents were talking about.

Now, it happened that when the father and mother reached home, they found a rich gentleman had sent them ten crowns, in payment for work, which had been done long before. The wife went out at once and bought bread and meat, and she and her husband sat down to make a hearty meal. But the mother could not forget her little ones; and at last she cried to her husband: "Alas, where are our poor children? How they would have enjoyed this good feast!"

The children, listening at the door, heard this and cried out, "Here we are, mother; here we are!" and, overjoyed, the mother flew to let them in and kissed them all round.

Spoken text uses quotation marks like these: " and are used for conversations in a story.

Exercises

1. Where does the story take place?

   A. on a mountain
   B. in a valley
   C. in the desert
   D. in the forest

CCSS.ELA-LITERACY.RL.1.1

2. What is the father's job?

   A. He is a woodcutter.
   B. He is a dentist.
   C. He is a blacksmith.
   D. He is a teacher.

CCSS.ELA-LITERACY.RL.1.3

3. In the story, what problem do the man and his wife have?

   A. Their house caught on fire.
   B. They do not have enough money or food.
   C. They are lost in the forest.
   D. They are being chased by a monster.

CCSS.ELA-LITERACY.RL.1.7

4. What do the parents give to the children?

   A. a crust of bread
   B. blueberries
   C. an egg
   D. a piece of cheese

CCSS.ELA-LITERACY.RL.1.3

5. What does Tom overhear?

CCSS.ELA-LITERACY.RL.1.2

6. How do the children find their way back home?

CCSS.ELA-LITERACY.RL.1.2

WEEK 8

VIDEO
EXPLANATIONS

Adjectives

CCSS.ELA-LITERACY.L.1.1.F

Warm, *kind*, *yellow*, *tall*, *fuzzy*, and *sour* are all describing words. We use describing words to give more information.

Describing words are called adjectives.

Adjectives help to to make our writing better.

Read the following sentences. Which one sounds more interesting? Which sentence gives you more information?

The puppy and the kitten played.

The small white fuzzy puppy and the tiny furry gray kitten played.

The second sentence gives you more information. After reading it, you can picture in your mind what the two animals look like.

Look at the second sentence again.

The small white fuzzy puppy and the tiny furry gray kitten played.

Which words in the sentence describe?

small white fuzzy tiny furry gray

These words are all adjectives.

Look at another example.

Julia's beautiful blonde hair had grown during the long hot summer.

Which words in the sentence describe?

beautiful blonde long hot

These words help you to picture what Julia looks like and what the summer was like too.

Let's practice!

Adjectives help to describe things that your senses would notice.
Your senses are: taste, sight, touch, hear, and smell.

Exercises

Look at each sentence below. Fill in the missing words with adjectives that will help paint a clear picture.

1. The ____________ bear walked in the ____________ forest.

CCSS.ELA-LITERACY.L.1.1.F

2. The ____________ teacher wrote with a ____________ marker.

CCSS.ELA-LITERACY.L.1.1.F

3. My ____________ brother loves to read ____________ books.

CCSS.ELA-LITERACY.L.1.1.F

4. Mr. Wilson cooks ____________ food for his ____________ family.

CCSS.ELA-LITERACY.L.1.1.F

5. Write a sentence below that describes you. Circle the adjectives in your sentence.

CCSS.ELA-LITERACY.L.1.1.F

6. Write a sentence below that describes your favorite place. Circle the adjectives in the sentence.

CCSS.ELA-LITERACY.L.1.1.F

Types of Adjectives

CCSS.ELA-LITERACY.L.1.1.F

There are three types of adjectives that can help you to describe your thoughts in detail.

Adjectives can describe (as we practiced before), they can tell about the quantity (number) of something, and they can answer the question: Which one?

Take a look at these examples:

Descriptive:	Quantitative:	Demonstrative:
small	three	that
tired	sixteen	this
purple	forty	those

Each type helps to make the information in a sentence more vivid, and allows you to paint a better picture about what is being shared.

Let's look at the difference between these three types.

Descriptive:

Jake held red balloons.

Quantitative:

Jake held three balloons.

Demonstrative:

Jake held those balloons.

Each sentence helps the reader to understand information about the balloons.

Let's practice!

Using these three different types of adjectives can make your writing even better. Try to use all three types when writing.

Exercises

Circle the adjective in each sentence. Then decide if the adjective is descriptive, demonstrative, or quantitative and write it on the line.

1. Her blue notebook was left at school.

CCSS.ELA-LITERACY.L.1.1.F

2. The cool water touched our toes.

CCSS.ELA-LITERACY.L.1.1.F

3. His three dogs slept in the sun.

CCSS.ELA-LITERACY.L.1.1.F

4. Maria chose that game to play.

CCSS.ELA-LITERACY.L.1.1.F

5. Jim loves to buy those cookies.

CCSS.ELA-LITERACY.L.1.1.F

6. My aunt has two days left to visit.

CCSS.ELA-LITERACY.L.1.1.F

Prepositions

CCSS.ELA-LITERACY.L.1.1.I

Prepositions help to share more information in sentences. Combined with adjectives, they can paint an even clearer picture for a reader.

A preposition is a word that connects a noun or pronoun to a verb or adjective in a sentence.

Prepositions can help to tell about direction, time, and place.

Look at the following examples.

Direction:	Time:	Place:
towards	during	on
through	in	at
down	from	between

The ball travelled *through* the air. (direction)
The ball travelled *during* the kickoff. (time)
The ball travelled *between* the bases. (place)

Let's practice!

A preposition is the first word in a prepositional phrase.

Exercises

Identify the prepositions in the sentences below and circle them.

1. Delaney swam in the water near the shore.

CCSS.ELA-LITERACY.L.1.1.I

2. The doctor listened to the patient at his office.

CCSS.ELA-LITERACY.L.1.1.I

3. I sing in the shower after my morning run.

CCSS.ELA-LITERACY.L.1.1.I

4. The snow fell on the ground during the storm.

CCSS.ELA-LITERACY.L.1.1.I

5. Bob's bike is by the garage at his house.

CCSS.ELA-LITERACY.L.1.1.I

6. We play with our friends at the park on the swings.

CCSS.ELA-LITERACY.L.1.1.I

WEEK 9

VIDEO
EXPLANATIONS

ARGOPREP.COM

Little Red Riding Hood

There was once a sweet little maid who lived with her father and mother in a pretty little cottage at the edge of the village. At the further end of the wood was another pretty cottage and in it lived her grandmother.

Everybody loved this little girl, her grandmother perhaps loved her most of all and gave her a great many pretty things. Once she gave her a red cloak with a hood which she always wore, so people called her Little Red Riding Hood.

One morning Little Red Riding Hood's mother said, "Put on your things and go to see your grandmother. She has been ill; take along this basket for her. I have put in it eggs, butter and cake, and other dainties."

It was a bright and sunny morning. Red Riding Hood was so happy that at first she wanted to dance through the wood. All around her grew pretty wild flowers which she loved so well and she stopped to pick a bunch for her grandmother.

Little Red Riding Hood wandered from her path and was stooping to pick a flower when from behind her a gruff voice said, "Good morning, Little Red Riding Hood." Little Red Riding Hood turned around and saw a great big wolf, but Little Red Riding Hood did not know what a wicked beast the wolf was, so she was not afraid.

"What have you in that basket, Little Red Riding Hood?"

"Eggs and butter and cake, Mr. Wolf."

"Where are you going with them, Little Red Riding Hood?"

"I am going to my grandmother, who is ill, Mr. Wolf."

"Where does your grandmother live, Little Red Riding Hood?"

"Along that path, past the wild rose bushes, then through the gate at the end of the wood, Mr. Wolf."

Then Mr. Wolf again said, "Good morning" and set off, and Little Red Riding Hood again went in search of wild flowers.

At last he reached the porch covered with flowers and knocked at the door of the cottage.

"Who is there?" called the grandmother.

"Little Red Riding Hood," said the wicked wolf.

"Press the latch, open the door, and walk in," said the grandmother.

The wolf pressed the latch, and walked in where the grandmother lay in bed. He made one jump at her, but she jumped out of bed into a closet. Then the wolf put on the cap which she had dropped and crept under the bedclothes.

In a short while Little Red Riding Hood knocked at the door, and walked in, saying, "Good morning, Grandmother, I have brought you eggs, butter and cake, and here is a bunch of flowers I gathered in the wood." As she came nearer the bed she said, "What big ears you have, Grandmother."

"All the better to hear you with, my dear."

This story is a fairy tale. Fairy tales happen long ago and usually have a hero or heroine in them.

"What big eyes you have, Grandmother."

"All the better to see you with, my dear."

"But, Grandmother, what a big nose you have."

"All the better to smell with, my dear."

"But, Grandmother, what a big mouth you have."

"All the better to eat you up with, my dear," he said as he sprang at Little Red Riding Hood.

Just at that moment Little Red Riding Hood's father was passing the cottage and heard her scream. He rushed in and with his axe chopped off Mr. Wolf's head. Everybody was happy that Little Red Riding Hood had escaped the wolf.

Then Little Red Riding Hood's father carried her home and they lived happily ever after.

Exercises

1. Where did Little Red Riding Hood's grandmother live?

   A. In the desert
   B. In a cottage
   C. In a mansion
   D. By a pond

   CCSS.ELA-LITERACY.RL.1.3

2. Which item was NOT mentioned in the basket?

   A. fruit
   B. butter
   C. cake
   D. eggs

   CCSS.ELA-LITERACY.RL.1.3

3. What did Little Red Riding Hood look for?

   A. wildflowers
   B. berries
   C. baby birds
   D. her kitten

   CCSS.ELA-LITERACY.RL.1.2

4. Where did the grandmother hide?

   A. Under the bed
   B. In her closet
   C. Behind the house
   D. On the porch

   CCSS.ELA-LITERACY.RL.1.3

5. Why is the girl called Little Red Riding Hood?

   A. Her favorite color is red.
   B. Her parents love the color red.
   C. She has red hair.
   D. She wears a red hooded cape.

   CCSS.ELA-LITERACY.RL.1.1

6. Who rescued Little Red Riding Hood?

   A. her grandmother
   B. her mother
   C. her father
   D. her brother

   CCSS.ELA-LITERACY.RL.1.3

Notes

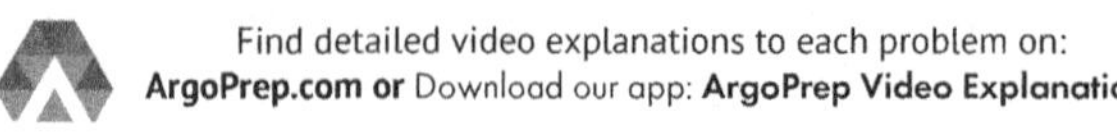

Teeny-Tiny

Once upon a time there was a teeny-tiny woman lived in a teeny-tiny house in a teeny-tiny village. Now, one day this teeny-tiny woman put on her teeny-tiny bonnet, and went out of her teeny-tiny house to take a teeny-tiny walk. And when this teeny-tiny woman had gone a teeny-tiny way she came to a teeny-tiny gate; so the teeny-tiny woman opened the teeny-tiny gate, and went into a teeny-tiny churchyard.

And when this teeny-tiny woman had got into the teeny-tiny churchyard, she saw a teeny-tiny bone on a teeny-tiny grave, and the teeny-tiny woman said to her teeny-tiny self, "This teeny-tiny bone will make me some teeny-tiny soup for my teeny-tiny supper." So the teeny-tiny woman put the teeny-tiny bone into her teeny-tiny pocket, and went home to her teeny-tiny house.

Now when the teeny-tiny woman got home to her teeny-tiny house she was a teeny-tiny bit tired; so she went up her teeny-tiny stairs to her teeny-tiny bed, and put the teeny-tiny bone into a teeny-tiny cupboard.

And when this teeny-tiny woman had been to sleep a teeny-tiny time, she was awakened by a teeny-tiny voice from the teeny-tiny cupboard, which said: "Give me my bone!" And this teeny-tiny woman was a teeny-tiny frightened, so she hid her teeny-tiny head under the teeny-tiny clothes and went to sleep again.

And when she had been to sleep again a teeny-tiny time, the teeny-tiny voice again cried out from the teeny-tiny cupboard a teeny-tiny louder, "Give me my bone!"

This made the teeny-tiny woman a teeny-tiny more frightened, so she hid her teeny-tiny head a teeny-tiny further under the teeny-tiny clothes.

And when the teeny-tiny woman had been to sleep again a teeny-tiny time, the teeny-tiny voice from the teeny-tiny cupboard said again a teeny-tiny louder, "Give me my bone!"

And this teeny-tiny woman was a teeny-tiny bit more frightened, but she put her teeny-tiny head out of the teeny-tiny clothes, and said in her loudest teeny-tiny voice, "TAKE IT!"

Do you notice a pattern in this story? Patterns can help you as you read.

Exercises

1. Where did the teeny-tiny woman go?

   A. Into a teeny-tiny office
   B. Into a teeny-tiny bank
   C. Into a teeny-tiny market
   D. Into a teeny-tiny churchyard

CCSS.ELA-LITERACY.RL.1.1

2. What does the teeny-tiny woman want to make?

   A. pie
   B. soup
   C. bread
   D. tea

CCSS.ELA-LITERACY.RL.1.3

3. What does the teeny-tiny woman put in her pocket?

   A. a bone
   B. money
   C. a note
   D. candy

CCSS.ELA-LITERACY.RL.1.3

4. What does the teeny-tiny woman hear?

   A. music
   B. a voice
   C. a barking dog
   D. a siren

CCSS.ELA-LITERACY.RL.1.4

5. How does the teeny-tiny woman feel before the end of the story?

   A. sad
   B. scared
   C. angry
   D. tired

CCSS.ELA-LITERACY.RL.1.3

6. Which word describes the final action of the teeny-tiny woman?

   A. silly
   B. brave
   C. hard
   D. quiet

CCSS.ELA-LITERACY.RL.1.3

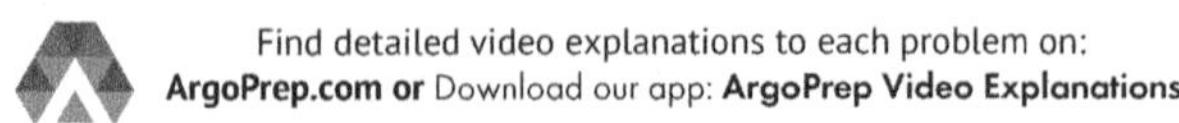

Excerpt from Rumpelstiltskin

By the side of a wood, in a country a long way off, ran a fine stream of water; and upon the stream there stood a mill. The miller's house was close by, and the miller, you must know, had a very beautiful daughter.

She was, moreover, very shrewd and clever; and the miller was so proud of her, that he one day told the king of the land, who used to come and hunt in the wood, that his daughter could spin gold out of straw.

Now this king was very fond of money; and when he heard the miller's boast his greediness was raised, and he sent for the girl to be brought before him. Then he led her to a chamber in his palace where there was a great heap of straw, and gave her a spinning-wheel, and said, "All this must be spun into gold before morning, as you love your life." It was in vain that the poor maiden said that it was only a silly boast of her father, for that she could do no such thing as spin straw into gold: the chamber door was locked, and she was left alone.

She sat down in one corner of the room, and began to bewail her hard fate; when on a sudden the door opened, and a droll-looking little man hobbled in, and said, "Good morrow to you, my good lass; what are you weeping for?"

"Alas!" said she, "I must spin this straw into gold, and I know not how."

"What will you give me," said the hobgoblin, "to do it for you?"

"My necklace," replied the maiden. He took her at her word, and sat himself down to the wheel, and whistled and sang:

"Round about, round about,
  Lo and behold!
Reel away, reel away,
  Straw into gold!"

And round about the wheel went merrily; the work was quickly done, and the straw was all spun into gold.

When the king came and saw this, he was greatly astonished and pleased; but his heart grew still more greedy of gain, and he shut up the poor miller's daughter again with a fresh task. Then she knew not what to do, and sat down once more to weep; but the dwarf soon opened the door, and said, "What will you give me to do your task?"

"The ring on my finger," said she.

The author describes the setting in great detail right away to help readers understand when and where the story happens.

Exercises

1. What did the man tell the king?

   A. His daughter could spin gold out of straw.
   B. His daughter could turn coal into diamonds.
   C. His daughter could make sand into silver.
   D. His daughter could turn water into money.

   CCSS.ELA-LITERACY.RL.1.1

2. What is the father's job?

   A. He is a woodcutter.
   B. He is a miller
   C. He is a blacksmith.
   D. He is a doctor.

   CCSS.ELA-LITERACY.RL.1.3

3. Which adjective describes the king?

   A. kind
   B. lazy
   C. greedy
   D. old

   CCSS.ELA-LITERACY.RL.1.7

4. What does the maiden offer to give away?

   A. her necklace
   B. her earrings
   C. her bracelet
   D. her pin

   CCSS.ELA-LITERACY.RL.1.3

5. Who helps the maiden?

   CCSS.ELA-LITERACY.RL.1.2

6. How does the king respond when he sees the gold?

   CCSS.ELA-LITERACY.RL.1.2

WEEK 10

VIDEO
EXPLANATIONS

ARGOPREP.COM

Singular and Plural Pronouns

CCSS.ELA-LITERACY.L.1.1.D

A pronoun takes the place of a noun. Some pronouns refer to one person or thing. Other pronouns refer to more than one person or thing.

Some examples of pronouns are: *he, him, she, her, they, them, we, us, our*

Look at the example below:

Courtney likes to go shopping.

She likes to go shopping.

The pronoun in the second sentence is the word *she.* The pronoun is singular and refers back to *Courtney.*

Look at the next example:

Leah and Allie play basketball on Wednesdays.

They play basketball on Wednesdays.

The pronoun in the second sentence is the word *They.* The pronoun is plural and refers back to *Leah and Allie.*

Here are some other commonly used singular pronouns:

I	me
you	him
herself	himself

Here are some other commonly used plural pronouns:

we	us
they	them
both	

Let's practice!

A pronoun always refers back to someone or something.

Exercises

Look at each sentence below. Circle the pronoun in each sentence. Decide if it is singular or plural and write the correct choice on the line.

1. She sang in the show.

CCSS.ELA-LITERACY.L.1.1.D

2. They go on vacation in July.

CCSS.ELA-LITERACY.L.1.1.D

3. We will leave in ten minutes.

CCSS.ELA-LITERACY.L.1.1.D

4. Brenda went with him to the mall.

CCSS.ELA-LITERACY.L.1.1.D

5. Brad looked for us at the park.

CCSS.ELA-LITERACY.L.1.1.D

6. The family plays basketball with them.

CCSS.ELA-LITERACY.L.1.1.D

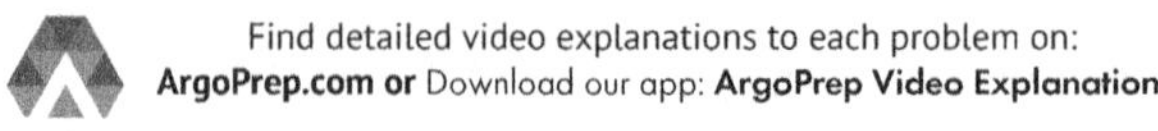

Subject and Object Pronouns

CCSS.ELA-LITERACY.L.1.1.D

There are two main types of pronouns.

Subject pronouns usually come before the verb and include I, he, she, you, it, we, and they.

Object pronouns usually come after the verb and take the place of a noun that receives the action. Object pronouns include me, you, him, her, them, us, and it.

Subject Pronoun:		Object Pronoun:
I		me
you		him
he	+ verb	her
she		you
it		it
we		us
they		them

Take a look at these examples to learn the difference between a subject pronoun and an object pronoun.

Madison sings to Bill.	She sings to him.
Tim loves ice cream.	He likes it.
The children play with the pets.	They play with them.

Remember: A subject pronoun comes before the verb, and an object pronoun comes after the verb.

Let's practice!

Remember to always include a person's name first before using the matching pronoun.

Exercises

Read each sentence. Circle the subject pronoun.

1. I hope to get there soon.

CCSS.ELA-LITERACY.L.1.1.D

2. She dreams about it often.

CCSS.ELA-LITERACY.L.1.1.D

3. We are angry about that.

CCSS.ELA-LITERACY.L.1.1.D

Read each sentence. Circle the object pronoun.

4. He can fly it.

CCSS.ELA-LITERACY.L.1.1.D

5. She lives with them.

CCSS.ELA-LITERACY.L.1.1.D

6. We clapped for them

CCSS.ELA-LITERACY.L.1.1.D

Possessive Pronouns

CCSS.ELA-LITERACY.L.1.1.D

Possessive pronouns show ownership.

mine	yours
theirs	ours
my	his
hers	its

Look at the examples below:

The dog wagged *its* tail.

Please return *my* pencil.

That is *your* paper.

My bike has a flat tire.

The pizza delivery is *mine*.

Notice that some possessive pronouns are located within the subject part of the sentence, while others are located within the predicate part of the sentence and function as an object.

Her smile is very pretty.	subject
The dogs are *theirs*.	object

Let's practice!

Pronouns can show possession. Did you notice that they do not use an apostrophe, unlike possessive nouns?

Exercises

Identify the possessive pronouns in the sentences below and circle them.

1. Her song was slow and pretty.

CCSS.ELA-LITERACY.L.1.1.D

2. Their principal walked near them in the hallway.

CCSS.ELA-LITERACY.L.1.1.D

3. Jane left with my papers.

CCSS.ELA-LITERACY.L.1.1.D

4. We gave the police officer our names.

CCSS.ELA-LITERACY.L.1.1.D

5. His tooth was hurting him all night.

CCSS.ELA-LITERACY.L.1.1.D

6. We listened to her directions.

CCSS.ELA-LITERACY.L.1.1.D

WEEK 11

VIDEO
EXPLANATIONS

ARGOPREP.COM

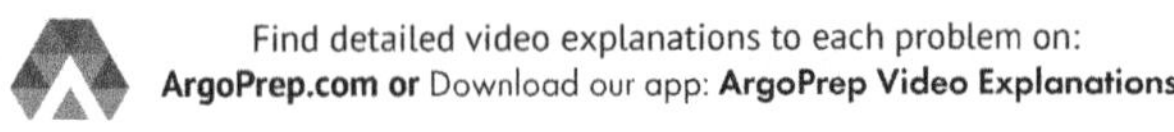

Chris Goes Camping

Under the stars, the rain fell. Chris hid and watched from his orange tent. His mom, dad, and brother slept soundly. He could hear the sounds of animals through the rain. He could not sleep.

Chris had been bored the entire camping trip so far. There was nothing interesting to do here.

As he finally started to fall asleep, he heard a sound near his tent. He sat up quickly and listened again. He could hear something in the grass. He felt his heart beat quickly. What should Chris do? His family was still soundly sleeping. He tried to wake them, but none of them awoke.

Slowly, he sat up and looked outside. A small baby bear cub was walking around, sniffing the grass with its nose to the ground. Chris was surprised.

The bear was all by itself. He looked again. Was the bear alone? Suddenly, Chris's worry turned into sadness. The little bear was all by itself. It looked hungry.

Quietly, Chris opened one of the family's coolers. There were a few near the tent. They wouldn't need all of that food anyway.

"I'll help that bear," Chris thought.

He pushed some of the food out onto the ground. The bear stopped and saw that the food was there. Chris watched and waited. What would the bear do? It started to eat. First it had the family's hotdog buns, then some watermelon, and then some cheese. The bear ate in the moonlight and he stopped to look around. Had the bear noticed Chris?

Chris looked over and saw a big shadow! He felt scared again. He opened his mouth to yell, but stopped. Another bear, the mother, had come over too. She noticed Chris. She didn't bother him. She began to eat too and the baby followed her.

They finished all of it, and then began to leave. She stopped and turned around, looking at Chris. He froze. She nodded at him, and Chris smiled. He watched them go, and then fell sound asleep.

Which of your senses did you use when reading to understand the setting?

Exercises

1. Where does the story take place?

   A. In a stadium
   B. In the woods
   C. At the beach
   D. In the desert

   CCSS.ELA-LITERACY.RL.1.1

2. Why isn't Chris happy about camping?

   A. It is very hot outside.
   B. He is bored.
   C. He hates insects.
   D. He wanted to go to the beach instead.

   CCSS.ELA-LITERACY.RL.1.3

3. What is the author's purpose for writing the story?

   A. To entertain
   B. To convince you to do something
   C. To teach you about how to cook food while camping
   D. To help you plan a camping trip

   CCSS.ELA-LITERACY.RL.1.3

4. What does Chris see by his tent?

   A. a moose
   B. a coyote
   C. a baby bear
   D. a monster

   CCSS.ELA-LITERACY.RL.1.3

5. Make a prediction. What will happen in the morning?

   A. Chris will tell his family what he saw.
   B. Chris will go back to his home.
   C. Chris will not want to leave the tent.
   D. Chris will take a trip to the beach.

   CCSS.ELA-LITERACY.RL.1.4

6. What word describes Chris in the story?

   A. kind
   B. funny
   C. proud
   D. selfish

   CCSS.ELA-LITERACY.RL.1.4

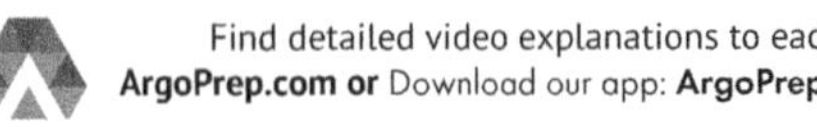

The Sea

Jessica couldn't wait to go on vacation. Her family was riding on a plane and going to an island. She would be able to play in the sand and water.

She had her suitcase packed and her family was ready to go. The pilot on the plane greeted them. Jessica sat near the window and looked outside.

She had been practicing her swimming at their pool and was eager to get into the clear warm water.

When they arrived, they checked into their huge hotel and had a bite to eat. They got ready for the beach and were greeted with sunshine and pretty birds flying overhead. With her flip flops on, Jessica made her way to the sand.

She got her towel ready and ran towards the water. That's when she noticed the big waves. Jessica had studied oceans in school. She had looked at postcards and pictures from her friends' trips. She had even watched shows and movies about the ocean, but she had never been to one before. She took a step back.

Again, she headed towards the water, but her mind was telling her to stop. Jessica was scared. The water was loud and the waves moved quickly.

Her brother came over to her.

"Let's go! What are you waiting for?" he asked. "Let's go for a swim!"

She shook her head no. She wasn't going near that water. She went back to her towel.

Each day, Jessica played in the sand. She made sandcastles and looked for shells. No matter how hot it was outside, she wouldn't go near the water.

On the last day of their trip, Jessica was feeling sad. Her brother knew why.

"I will stay with you in the water. Let's walk out and you can stop as soon as you want to. You are missing out on the best part of the beach," he said.

Jessica thought about it. She remembered stories from her friends about how much they loved to swim in the ocean.

She nodded. It was now or never, and she was ready to go for it!

Did the ending surprise you? Thinking about a new ending for stories you like is a great way to practice your creative writing skills.

Exercises

1. Where does Jessica's family go?

   A. to the beach
   B. to the desert
   C. to the movies
   D. to the store

CCSS.ELA-LITERACY.RL.1.3

2. What is the job of a pilot?

   A. A pilot flies a plane.
   B. A pilot controls a train.
   C. A pilot fixes cars.
   D. A pilot drives trucks.

CCSS.ELA-LITERACY.RL.1.3

3. How does Jessica feel about the water when she first sees it?

   A. It makes her feel happy.
   B. It makes her feel sad.
   C. It makes her feel angry.
   D. It makes her feel scared.

CCSS.ELA-LITERACY.RL.1.1

4. What does Jessica spend most of the trip doing?

   A. swimming and running
   B. collecting seashells and building sandcastles
   C. talking and singing
   D. reading and drawing

CCSS.ELA-LITERACY.RL.1.3

5. Who helps Jessica?

   A. her mom
   B. her dad
   C. her brother
   D. her sister

CCSS.ELA-LITERACY.RL.1.3

6. What might happen next?

   A. Jessica will go for a swim.
   B. Jessica will learn to fish.
   C. Jessica will build a sandcastle.
   D. Jessica will eat lunch.

CCSS.ELA-LITERACY.RL.1.1

On a Walk

Lauren and Alicia live in a big neighborhood. They love to ride bikes together, play at the park together, and draw with sidewalk chalk together.

It is almost the end of the summer, and both girls are bored. School starts next week in September. Alicia looks forward to her birthday the same week too.

They decide to go for a walk. On their way around the neighborhood, they notice painted rocks on the ground.

Bending down, Alicia picks one up. It has a letter S on the bottom of it and a number. It says: 1 out of 9.

Alicia shows it to Lauren. She smiles.

"Let's see if we can find some more!"

The girls continue on. They look near the sidewalk and flowerbeds. They look by the park and near mailboxes. They pick up a pink and yellow rock, a green rock, a blue and orange rock, and striped rocks.

They keep walking along, with eight in hand so far. They have one more to find.

"Where might the last one be?"

They girls look and look. They are now almost back to their houses, and have gone through the entire neighborhood.

Just then, Alicia spots it.

"There it is!" she yells.

It was right next to her mailbox.

"I didn't see this here before! Let's put them in order."

The girls begin to arrange them, putting them in order.

S-U-R-P-R-I-S-E-!

"What does it say?" Alicia asks. Then she reads it for herself.

"SURPRISE!" Lauren says, smiling.

Just then, Alicia's family and friends come into the yard. "SURPRISE!" they yell.

"It's not my birthday today!" Alicia says.

"It isn't today, but it IS next week, and this was a great way to make sure our secret stayed safe. Happy Birthday, Alicia!"

The girls enjoyed cake, ice cream, balloons, and fun with all of their friends. It was the perfect way to end the summer!

Why did the author include information in the beginning about Alicia's upcoming birthday? Small clues can become an important part of a story.

Exercises

1. What is wrong with the girls?

   A. They are hungry.
   B. They are tired.
   C. They are bored.
   D. They are lost.

CCSS.ELA-LITERACY.RL.1.1

2. What do they decide to do?

   A. draw with chalk
   B. take a walk
   C. ride their bikes
   D. rollerblade

CCSS.ELA-LITERACY.RL.1.3

3. What does Alicia find?

   A. a painted rock
   B. a lost dog
   C. a cake
   D. a balloon

CCSS.ELA-LITERACY.RL.1.4

4. How many items do they collect?

   A. 7
   B. 8
   C. 9
   D. 10

CCSS.ELA-LITERACY.RL.1.7

5. What word did they see when they put all of the items in order?

CCSS.ELA-LITERACY.RL.1.3

6. What happened at the end of the story? How did the girls both feel?

CCSS.ELA-LITERACY.RL.1.2

WEEK 12

VIDEO
EXPLANATIONS

Fragments and Declarative Sentences

CCSS.ELA-LITERACY.L.1.1J

A sentence shares a complete idea. **There are four types of sentences.**

During this lesson, we will take a close look at telling sentences. **Telling sentences are also known as declarative sentences.** Their job is to share a complete idea.

Remember that a sentence ends with a period, a small dot, after the last word.

You can give information with the use of nouns, verbs, adjectives, and many of the parts of speech we have already learned about so far.

Here are some examples:

We explored the pretty seashells in the clear water under the hot sun.

This is a complete thought and explains what the people are doing. It lets you picture in your mind the actions that are taking place.

Alyssa and Roman saw many large wild animals during their long safari in Africa.

This is a complete thought and explains what Alyssa and Roman saw. It lets you picture their safari in your mind.

All of these sentences share a complete idea.

Sometimes, a thought is incomplete. It might be missing a subject or a verb. This type of thought is known as a fragment.

Here are some examples:

In the ocean

Because it is snowing

How she has time for

None of these thoughts are complete. (Be careful! Sometimes incomplete thoughts have a period after them, even though they are not sentences.)

Let's fix the above examples and make them into declarative sentences:

In the ocean, we swim and play volleyball together.

Because it is snowing, I won't be able to get to my game on time.

How she has time for dance, softball, chess club, and homework, I will never understand.

Declarative sentences have a subject and a verb. They share a complete thought and end with a period.

Let's practice!

A sentence must have at least one subject and one verb. If not, it is an incomplete sentence.

Exercises

Look at each group of words. If it is a declarative thought, add the correct ending mark. If it is NOT a declarative thought, add some information, and then include the correct ending mark.

1. Melissa and Ben love to shop

CCSS.ELA-LITERACY.L.1.1.J

2. However you look at it

CCSS.ELA-LITERACY.L.1.1.J

3. Because I love the hot weather

CCSS.ELA-LITERACY.L.1.1.J

4. Whenever you get here

CCSS.ELA-LITERACY.L.1.1.J

5. I live in Texas

CCSS.ELA-LITERACY.L.1.1.J

6. My mother loves it

CCSS.ELA-LITERACY.L.1.1.J

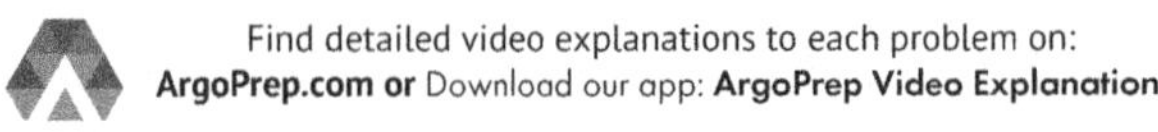

Interrogative Sentences

CCSS.ELA-LITERACY.L.1.1J

We can share complete ideas in the form of a question too. **These asking sentences are known as interrogative sentences.** Interrogative sentences are another type of sentence.

During this lesson, we will take a close look at how to ask a question as a complete thought.

Remember that when asking a question, the thought should end with a question mark after the last word. (?)

Questions often begin with the words **why**, **what**, **how**, **where**, **who, whom**, or **when**. Look for these key words to help you decide if a thought is an interrogative sentence.

Here are some examples:

What time should we leave to go to school?

This is a complete thought and asks a question. It uses the keyword *what* and ends with a question mark.

How did you do on your math test today?

This is a complete thought and asks a question. It uses the keyword *how* and ends with a question mark.

Both of these thoughts share a complete idea in the form of a question.

Interrogative sentences ask a question and are looking for information. They have a subject and a verb, share a complete thought, and end with a question mark.

Let's practice!

To interrogate someone means to ask him or her questions.
This can help you to remember what the word interrogative means.

Exercises

Look at each group of words. Complete each one in the form of an interrogative thought. Be sure to include a question mark at the end.

1. What day

CCSS.ELA-LITERACY.L.1.1.J

2. When will you

CCSS.ELA-LITERACY.L.1.1.J

3. How can I

CCSS.ELA-LITERACY.L.1.1.J

4. Who will

CCSS.ELA-LITERACY.L.1.1.J

5. When does she

CCSS.ELA-LITERACY.L.1.1.J

6. Where is

CCSS.ELA-LITERACY.L.1.1.J

Exclamatory and Imperative Sentences

CCSS.ELA-LITERACY.L.1.1J

We can share complete ideas when we are excited too. **These sentences are known as exclamatory sentences.** They end with an exclamation mark. This reminds the reader that the thought should be read with excitement. **Remember that an exclamation mark or exclamation point looks like this: !**

Think of something you have been excited about. Form a complete thought that tells about it. Does your thought make more sense with an exclamation point after it, or with another ending mark?

Look at the difference between these two thoughts.

Disney Land is my favorite place in the entire world.

Disney Land is my favorite place in the entire world!

Which thought helps to show excitement?

Using an exclamation point makes a big difference in sharing a thought.

Here are some examples of exclamatory sentences:

How thrilled I am to be able to travel the world!

This is a complete thought and uses an exclamation point to show excitement. It ends with an exclamation mark.

Our team won the championship today!

This is a complete thought and also uses an exclamation point to show excitement. It ends with an exclamation mark.

Exclamatory sentences share exciting information. They have a subject and a verb, share a complete thought, and end with an exclamation mark.

One additional sentence type often ends in an exclamation mark too. Sometimes our thoughts are shared in the form of a command.

A command tells someone to do something. **This type of sentence is known as an imperative sentence.**

Here are some examples of imperative sentences:

Go clean your room!

Please take out the trash soon!

Imperative sentences may also end with a period.

Here are some additional examples:

Put your pencil down.

Stand next to him.

Imperative sentences tell someone to do something. They have a subject and a verb, share a complete command, and end with an exclamation mark or a period.

Let's practice!

You now know four types of sentences. Try to incorporate all four types into a conversation with a friend today.

Exercises

Look at each group of words. Complete each one in the form of an imperative thought. Be sure to include an ending mark at the end in the form of an exclamation mark or a period.

1. Please go

CCSS.ELA-LITERACY.L.1.1.J

2. You need to

CCSS.ELA-LITERACY.L.1.1.J

3. Let's take

CCSS.ELA-LITERACY.L.1.1.J

4. I want you to

CCSS.ELA-LITERACY.L.1.1.J

5. Put your

CCSS.ELA-LITERACY.L.1.1.J

6. Stand next to

CCSS.ELA-LITERACY.L.1.1.J

WEEK 13

VIDEO EXPLANATIONS

ARGOPREP.COM

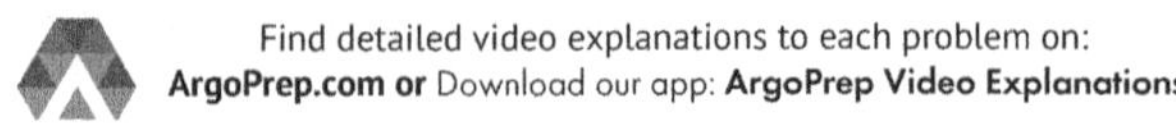

The Three Wishes

Once upon a time a poor man took his ax and went out into the forest to cut wood. He was a lazy fellow, so as soon as he was in the forest he began to look about to see which tree would be the easiest to cut down. At last he found one that was hollow inside, as he could tell by knocking upon it with his ax. "It ought not to take long to cut this down," said he to himself. He raised his ax and struck the tree such a blow that the splinters flew.

At once the bark opened and a little old fairy with a long beard came running out of the tree.

"What do you mean by chopping into my house?" he cried; and his eyes shone like red hot sparks, he was so angry.

"I did not know it was your house," said the man.

"Well, it is my house, and I'll thank you to let it alone," cried the fairy.

"Very well," said the man. "I'd just as I've cut down some other tree.

I'll chop down the one over yonder."

"That is well," said the fairy. "I see that you are an obliging fellow, after all. I have it in my mind to reward you for sparing my house, so the next three wishes you and your wife make shall come true, whatever they are; and that is your reward."

Then the fairy went back into the tree again and pulled the bark together behind him.

The man stood looking at the tree and scratching his head. "Now that is a curious thing," said he. Then he sat down and began to wonder what he should wish for. He thought and he thought, but he could decide on nothing. "I'll just go home and talk it over with my wife," said he; so he shouldered his ax, and set off for home. As soon as he came in at the door he began to bawl for his wife, and she came in a hurry, for she did not know what had happened to him.

He told his story and his wife listened. "This is a fine thing to have happen to us," said she. "Now we must be very careful what we wish for."

They sat down one on each side of the fire to talk it over. They thought of ever so many things they would like to have—a bag of gold, and a coach and four horses, and a fine house to live in, and fine clothes to wear, but nothing seemed just the right thing to choose.

They talked so long that they grew hungry. "Well, here we sit," said the man, "and not a thing cooked for dinner. I wish we had one of those fine black puddings you used to make."

No sooner had he spoken than there was a great thumping and bumping in the chimney and a great black pudding fell down on the hearth before him.

"What is this?" cried the man staring.

"Oh, you oaf! You're stupid!" shrieked his wife. "It's the pudding you wished for. There's one of our wishes wasted. I wish the pudding were stuck on the end of your nose! It would serve you right!"

This is a make believe story. It contains characters that cannot exist and things that cannot really happen.

The moment she said this the pudding flew up and stuck to the man's nose, and there it was and he couldn't get it off; the man pulled and tugged, and his wife pulled and tugged, but it was all of no use.

"Well, there's no help for it," said the husband; "we'll have to wish it off again."

His wife began to cry and bawl. "No, no," she cried. "We only have one wish left, and we can't waste it that way. Let's wish ourselves the richest people in the world."

But to this the man would not agree. He wanted the pudding off his nose whatever it cost. So at last the wife was obliged to let him have his own way. "I wish the pudding was off my nose again," said the man, and that was the third of their wishes. So all the good they had of the fairy's gift was a black pudding for dinner; but then it was the best black pudding they had ever eaten. "And after all," said the man, "there's nothing much better in the world to wish for than a full stomach."

Exercises

1. What does the man take to the forest?

   A. food
   B. a bow and arrow
   C. an ax
   D. his dog

   CCSS.ELA-LITERACY.RL.1.1

2. Who surprises him?

   A. a fairy
   B. a monster
   C. his wife
   D. his dog

   CCSS.ELA-LITERACY.RL.1.1

3. Why does his wife become angry?

   A. He is late for dinner.
   B. She cannot find him.
   C. He didn't chop down a tree.
   D. He wishes for pudding.

   CCSS.ELA-LITERACY.RL.1.3

4. What wish does the wife hope for?

   A. pudding
   B. riches
   C. a new pet
   D. a new home

   CCSS.ELA-LITERACY.RL.1.3

5. Which adjective might describe the wife at the end of the story?

   A. lost
   B. disappointed
   C. scared
   D. tired

   CCSS.ELA-LITERACY.RL.1.3

6. What did the couple receive?

   A. a lot of money
   B. the best pudding they had ever eaten
   C. a new mansion
   D. endless wishes

   CCSS.ELA-LITERACY.RL.1.2

Notes

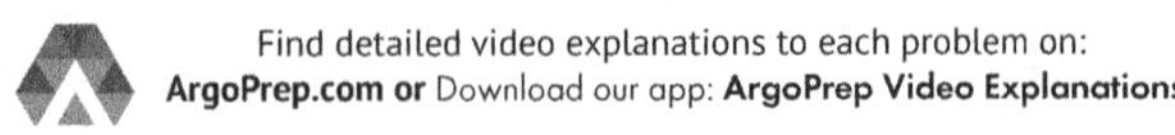

Chicken-Diddle

One day Chicken-diddle had gone to sleep under a rosebush, and a cow reached over the fence and bit off the top of the rosebush. The noise wakened Chicken-diddle, and just as she woke a rose leaf fell on her tail.

"Squawk! Squawk!" cried Chicken-diddle, "the sky's falling down;" and away she ran as fast as her legs would carry her. She ran until she came to the barnyard, and there was Hen-pen rustling in the dust of the barnyard.

"Oh, Hen-pen, don't rustle—run, run!" cried Chicken-diddle. "The sky's falling down."

The hen stopped rustling. "How do you know that Chicken-diddle?" asked Hen-pen.

"I saw it with my eyes, I heard it with my ears, and part of it fell on my tail. Oh, let us run, run, until we get some place."

"Quawk! Quawk," cried the hen, and she began to run, and Chicken-diddle ran after her.

They ran till they came to the duck-pond, and there was Duck-luck just going in for a swim.

"Oh, Duck-luck! Duck-luck! Don't try to swim," cried Hen-pen. "The sky's falling down."

"How do you know that, Hen-pen?" asked Duck-luck.

"Chicken-diddle told me."

"How do you know that, Chicken-diddle?"

"Why shouldn't I know it? I saw it with my eyes, I heard it with my ears, and part of it fell on my tail. Oh, let us run, run until we get some place."

"Yes, we had better run," quacked Duck-luck, and away he waddled with Hen-pen, and Chicken-diddle after him.

They ran and ran till they came to a green meadow, and there was Goose-loose eating the green grass.

"Oh, Goose-loose, Goose-loose, don't eat; run, run," cried Duck-luck.

"Why should I run?" asked Goose-loose.

"Because the sky's falling down."

"How do you know that, Duck-luck?"

"Hen-pen told me."

"How do you know that, Hen-pen?"

"Chicken-diddle told me."

"How do you know that, Chicken-diddle?"

"Because I saw it with my eyes, and heard it with my ears, and part of it fell on my tail. Oh, let us run, run some place."

What do most of the character names in the story have in common? They all follow the same name pattern. Why do you think the author did this?

"Yes, we'd better run," cried Goose-loose.

Away they all ran, Goose-loose at the head of them, and they ran and ran until they came to the turkey-yard, and there was Turkey-lurkey strutting and gobbling.

"Oh, Turkey-lurkey! Don't strut! Don't strut!" cried Goose-loose.

"Why should I not strut?" asked Turkey-lurkey.

"Because the sky's falling down."

"How do you know it is?"

"Duck-luck told me!"

"How do you know, Duck-luck?"

"Hen-pen told me!"

"How do you know, Hen-pen?"

"Chicken-diddle told me!"

"How do you know, Chicken-diddle?"

"I couldn't help knowing! I saw it with my eyes, I heard it with my ears, and a part of it fell on my tail. Oh, let us run, run until we get some place."

"Yes, we'd better run," said Turkey-lurkey, so away they all ran, first

Turkey-lurkey, and then Goose-loose, and then Duck-luck, and then Hen-pen, and then Chicken-diddle.

They ran and ran until they came to Fox-lox's house, and there was

Fox-lox lying in the doorway and yawning until his tongue curled up in his mouth. When he saw Turkey-lurkey and Goose-loose and Duck-luck and Hen-pen and Chicken-diddle he stopped yawning, and pricked up his ears, and he was very glad to see them.

"Well, well," said he, "and what brings you all here?"

"Oh, Fox-lox, Fox-lox, don't yawn," cried Turkey-lurkey, "the sky's falling down."

"How do you know that, Turkey-lurkey?" asked the fox.

"Goose-loose told me."

"How do you know that, Goose-loose?"

"Duck-luck told me."

"How do you know that, Duck-luck?"

"Hen-pen told me."

"How do you know that, Hen-pen?"

"Chicken-diddle told me."

"How do you know that, Chicken-diddle?"

"I couldn't help knowing, for I saw it with my eyes, and I heard it with my ears, and part of it fell on my tail. Oh, where shall we run?

We ought to go some place."

"Well," said the Fox, "you come right in here, and I'll take such good care of you that even if the sky falls down you won't know anything about it."

So in ran Turkey-lurkey, and Fox-lox put him in the big room, and shut the door. In ran Goose-loose, and he put him in the little room, and shut the door. In ran Duck-luck, and he put him in the cellar, and shut the door. In ran Hen-pen, and he put her in the attic, and shut the door. In ran Chicken-diddle, and Fox-lox kept him right there in the room with him. And what happened to them after that I don't know, but nobody ever saw them again; if the sky really fell, I never heard about it. They were only a pack of silly fowls, anyway.

Why doesn't the fox's name follow the same pattern as the other characters?

1. Why is Chicken-diddle worried?

   A. She is lost.
   B. The sky is falling down.
   C. She cannot find food.
   D. The chicken coop is too crowded.

CCSS.ELA-LITERACY.RL.1.3

2. What does Duck-luck think they should do?

   A. run
   B. hide
   C. sleep
   D. move away

CCSS.ELA-LITERACY.RL.1.3

3. Where does Turkey-lurkey go?

   A. With the chickens in the coop
   B. With the ducks to the pond
   C. With the other turkeys into the woods
   D. With the fox into his room

CCSS.ELA-LITERACY.RL.1.1

4. What happened to the other animals?

   A. They found the farmer who helped them.
   B. They travelled to the next town.
   C. They were tricked by Fox-lox.
   D. They became angry with one another.

CCSS.ELA-LITERACY.RL.1.3

5. What word describes Fox-lox?

   A. lazy
   B. angry
   C. tired
   D. clever

CCSS.ELA-LITERACY.RL.1.3

6. Which word is a synonym for the word *fowls*?

   A. birds
   B. eggs
   C. mammals
   D. predators

CCSS.ELA-LITERACY.RL.1.4

The Golden Key

It was winter, and a little lad had gone out into the forest to gather wood to keep the fire going at home. As there was snow upon the ground he took his little sledge with him, for he could carry home a larger load on the sledge than on his back.

He gathered together a heap of fallen branches, and then piled them neatly on the sledge, putting the larger pieces at the bottom. Before he had finished the task his fingers were almost frozen, for he had no mittens. "Before I start to drag my sled home," said he to himself, "I will build a fire and warm my hands a bit."

He took a stick, and cleared away some of the snow, so as to have a place to build the fire. When he had done this he saw a little golden key lying there on the ground. The little lad picked it up, wondering.

"Wherever there is a key, there must be a lock," he said.

He began to scrape away the earth, and presently he found a curious looking chest made of iron inlaid with silver. There were words written on the lid of the chest, but the little boy could not read them.

He lifted the chest out from the earth, and it seemed to him that something was stirring inside of it. Then a little thin voice, as thin as a thread, cried to him. "Let me out! Let me out, and I will make your fortune."

The little boy was very much surprised. The chest seemed too small for any living being to be in it.

"Who are you?" he asked.

"Open the chest and see. If you will only let me out you will never be sorry."

The little boy put the golden key in the lock and it fitted exactly. He turned it round and the lock flew back. But as to what was in the chest you will have to wait until he lifts the lid before you can see.

The author includes the season in the first sentence of the story. Think about why this is important.

Exercises

1. Which word is a synonym for the word *lad*?

   A. boy
   B. baby
   C. girl
   D. son

CCSS.ELA-LITERACY.RL.1.1

2. Where does the lad go?

   A. to the sea
   B. to school
   C. to the forest
   D. to his home

CCSS.ELA-LITERACY.RL.1.3

3. What does the lad want to build?

   A. a house
   B. a birdhouse
   C. a raft
   D. a fire

CCSS.ELA-LITERACY.RL.1.4

4. What does he unexpectedly find?

   A. a golden key
   B. a fairy
   C. a monster
   D. gold coins

CCSS.ELA-LITERACY.RL.1.7

5. What did the boy search for?

CCSS.ELA-LITERACY.RL.1.3

6. What might be in the chest?

CCSS.ELA-LITERACY.RL.1.2

WEEK 14

VIDEO
EXPLANATIONS

ARGOPREP.COM

Find detailed video explanations to each problem on:
ArgoPrep.com or Download our app: **ArgoPrep Video Explanations**

Commas in a Series

CCSS.ELA-LITERACY.L.1.2.C

Commas are used for many reasons. When we share complete thoughts, sometimes we list many items in a row. **We use commas to separate them. A comma looks like this: , and** it can help to make our ideas clear.

A series is a group of three or more adjectives, people, places, or things.

Here are some examples:

We went to the store, the park, and the ice cream shop after lunch.

This is a complete thought and lists three places that the subject went. The places listed are: the store, the park, and the ice cream shop.

Without commas, the sentence would look like this instead:

We went to the store the park and the ice cream shop after lunch.

Without commas, the information is not clear to the reader.

Another example:

Jennifer eats lunch with Ray, Bill, Jessica, Mary Beth, and Lynn.

This is a complete thought and lists the five people that Jennifer eats lunch with. The people listed are: Ray, Bill, Jessica, Mary Beth, Lynn.

Without commas, the sentence would look like this instead:

Jennifer eats lunch with Ray Bill Jessica Mary Beth and Lynn.

Without commas, the information is not clear to the reader.

One more example:

She was delighted, surprised, proud, and thankful all at the same time.

This is a complete thought and lists the four adjectives. The adjectives listed are: delighted, surprised, proud, thankful.

Without commas, the sentence would look like this instead:

She was delighted surprised proud and thankful all at the same time.

Without commas, the information is not clear to the reader.

Commas are used to separate items in a series and help to make thoughts clear.

Let's practice!

If you have four items in a series, you will use three commas. If you have five items in a series, you will use four commas. Use this pattern to help you when you write.

Exercises

Look at the sentences. Add commas where needed and write the sentence correctly on the line.

1. My favorite colors are orange yellow and blue.

CCSS.ELA-LITERACY.L.1.2.C

2. Remember to pack shirts socks and shoes for the trip.

CCSS.ELA-LITERACY.L.1.2.C

3. I love to draw color and write in my notebook.

CCSS.ELA-LITERACY.L.1.2.C

4. Lunch is after math science gym and English.

CCSS.ELA-LITERACY.L.1.2.C

5. I have gone to Texas Florida New York and Ohio.

CCSS.ELA-LITERACY.L.1.2.C

6. My dad brother sister and I will all be there.

CCSS.ELA-LITERACY.L.1.2.C

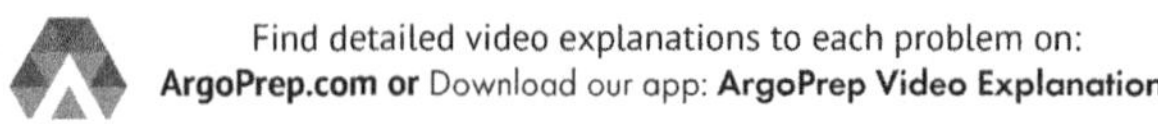

Commas with introductions

CCSS.ELA-LITERACY.L.1.2.C

Commas are used when introducing a thought. When you read a sentence aloud and pause, this is often where a comma should go.

A comma looks like this: , and it can help to make our ideas clear.

Introductory phrases share the beginning of a thought.

Here are some examples:

After leaving the zoo, we decided to go to the store.

This is a complete thought with an introduction. There is a natural pause in the sentence. This is where a comma should fit.

Here are some more examples:

While running outside, Katie noticed birds around her.

Because she loved to bake, Maria was in the kitchen a lot.

During the movie, Michael ate popcorn.

Notice the introductory phrase in each one:

While running outside,

Because she loved to bake,

During the movie,

The comma after each phrase lets you know that more information is coming.

Let's practice!

TIP of the DAY

An introduction sets the tone for the sentence.

Exercises

Look at the sentences. Add commas where needed and write the sentence correctly on the line.

1. Before going to see the dentist brush and floss your teeth.

CCSS.ELA-LITERACY.L.1.2.C

2. After she got on the airplane she waved from the window.

CCSS.ELA-LITERACY.L.1.2.C

3. Upon finding the lost key Jenny clapped her hands and cheered.

CCSS.ELA-LITERACY.L.1.2.C

4. While eating her lunch Aubrie watched the people walking by.

CCSS.ELA-LITERACY.L.1.2.C

5. Under the sea there are many types of fish to look at.

CCSS.ELA-LITERACY.L.1.2.C

6. On Maple Street Judy and her brother visit their cousins.

CCSS.ELA-LITERACY.L.1.2.C

Commas in dates, locations, and in friendly letters

CCSS.ELA-LITERACY.L.1.2.C

Commas are also used in a few other ways like when we write dates on our school papers or in a letter.

When a date is written out using words, a comma is placed within it.

Let's take a look at some examples.

March 5, 2019

September 20, 2011

December 13, 1998

Notice the comma that comes before the year.

Commas are also used when separating a city from a state, like this:

Orlando, Florida

Boise, Idaho

Las Vegas, Nevada

San Francisco, California

Lastly, **commas are also used in introductions and closings in letters.**

Take a look at these examples:

Dear Mary,

Best regards,
Julie Smith

Fondly,
John

Sincerely,
Mrs. Miller

Let's practice!

Practice using commas by writing a letter to a friend or family member. Include a date and closing.

Exercises

Add a comma where needed in the examples below.

1. July 14 2017

CCSS.ELA-LITERACY.L.1.2.C

2. Dear Annabelle

CCSS.ELA-LITERACY.L.1.2.C

3. Pittsburgh Pennsylvania

CCSS.ELA-LITERACY.L.1.2.C

4. New York City New York

CCSS.ELA-LITERACY.L.1.2.C

5. Dearest Rachel

CCSS.ELA-LITERACY.L.1.2.C

6. Sincerely
Robert Denton

CCSS.ELA-LITERACY.L.1.2.C

WEEK 15

VIDEO EXPLANATIONS

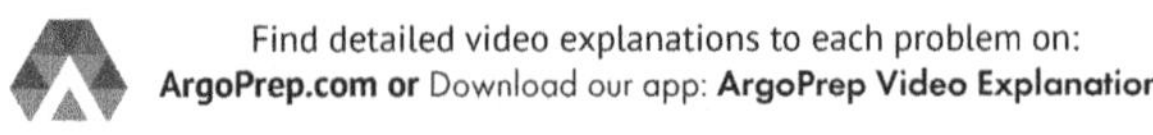

The Nail

A merchant had been trading in a far city and had made much money, which he was now bringing home with him. He rode in haste, for he knew he would not feel easy until he had locked away the gold in his strong room at home.

Toward the middle of the morning he stopped at an inn to give his horse water. "Sir," said the ostler who waited on him, "a nail is loose in your horse's shoe."

"No matter," answered the merchant. "I am in haste, and the shoe must go as it is till I get home."

A little later he stopped at another inn. "Sir," said the ostler, "your horse's shoe is loose; shall I not take him to the blacksmith near by and have the shoe fastened on?"

"No," answered the merchant, "I have not time to wait. I must be home before nightfall."

The merchant rode still farther, but presently his horse began to limp. It limped more and more, until at last, in the very midst of a deep forest, it stumbled and fell, and could not get up again.

The merchant was in despair. Dusk was coming on, and there seemed nothing for it but to spend the night in the forest. However, he discovered a house near by, and the old woman who was in charge of it promised him food and a lodging for the night.

When the merchant went up to bed he put his bag of gold under his pillow. He meant to watch all night, but he was very tired, and presently, in spite of himself his eyes closed and he fell into a deep sleep.

Now this house belonged to a band of robbers, and the old woman was their housekeeper. Soon after the merchant was asleep the robbers came home. The housekeeper told them of the rich man who had come to the house while they were away, and of how she had given him a bed for the night.

The robbers went up to the merchant's room and finding him asleep they stole the bag of money from under his pillow, and made off with it.

In the morning, when the merchant awoke, he felt under his pillow for the bag, but it was gone. He called aloud, but no one answered. He searched the house from top to bottom, but could find nobody.

So the merchant lost both his gold and his horse. "And all," said he, "because I was in such haste that I would not stop for a nail to be put in my horse's shoe. It is a true saying – 'the more haste the less speed.'"

When you come across an unknown vocabulary word, write it down so that you can check your understanding of it after reading.

Exercises

1. Where is the merchant heading to in the beginning of the story?

   A. the city
   B. his home
   C. the beach
   D. to see the king

   CCSS.ELA-LITERACY.RL.1.1

2. What problem does the merchant have?

   A. His horse's hoof needs fixed.
   B. He has a flat tire.
   C. He doesn't feel well.
   D. He lost his money.

   CCSS.ELA-LITERACY.RL.1.3

3. Why is the merchant trying to hurry?

   A. He wants to see his wife.
   B. He wants to get some food.
   C. He want to get his horse to the vet.
   D. He wants to lock up his gold.

   CCSS.ELA-LITERACY.RL.1.3

4. What word might describe the merchant?

   A. impatient
   B. kind
   C. intelligent
   D. sly

   CCSS.ELA-LITERACY.RL.1.3

5. Where does the merchant fall asleep?

   A. in his own bed
   B. in a house in the forest
   C. at a hotel
   D. on the ground

   CCSS.ELA-LITERACY.RL.1.4

6. What happens to his gold?

   A. Someone takes it from under his pillow.
   B. He locks it up in a safe and loses the key.
   C. He gives it to the king.
   D. He loses it on the ground in the forest.

   CCSS.ELA-LITERACY.RL.1.4

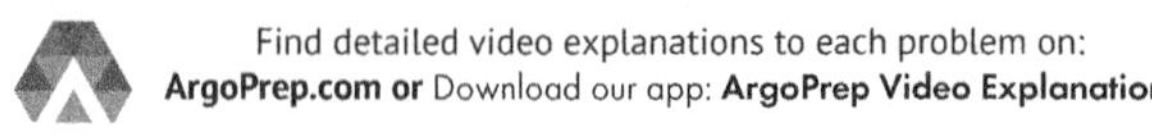

An Excerpt from Cinderella

There was once a girl named Ella who was so gentle and beautiful that everyone who knew her loved her, except those who should have loved her best, and those were her stepmother and her stepsisters.

Her own mother had died while she was quite young, and then her father had married again. This new wife had two daughters of her own, and she wished them to have everything and Ella to have nothing. The stepmother dressed her own children in fine clothes, and they sat about and did nothing all day, but Cinderella worked in the kitchen and had nothing but rags to wear, and because she often sat close to the ashes to warm herself her sisters called her Cinderella.

Now the King and Queen of that country had only one son, and they were very anxious for him to marry, but he had never seen anyone whom he wished to have for a bride. At last they determined to give a great ball, and to ask to it all the fairest ladies in the land. They hoped that among them all, the Prince might see someone whom he would choose.

All the grand people of the city were invited, and Cinderella's stepmother and her stepsisters were asked with all the rest.

The stepsisters were very much excited over it. They were both so handsome that they hoped one of them might be chosen by the Prince. They had often watched from the windows to see him riding by, and he was so gallant that anyone might have been glad to marry him.

All sorts of fine things were bought for the sisters to wear, satins and velvets and laces and jewels, feathers for their hair, and glittering fans for them to carry, and the stepmother's dress was no less fine than theirs.

Cinderella sighed and sighed. "I wish I might go to the ball, too, and see that handsome Prince and all the lovely ladies," she said.

"You!" cried the sisters, laughing. "A pretty sight you would be at the ball; you with your rags and your sooty hands."

Why might the author use the names Ella and Cinderella to refer to the same character?

Exercises

1. Who is the main character in the story?

   A. the Queen
   B. Ella
   C. the King
   D. the eldest stepsister

CCSS.ELA-LITERACY.RL.1.3

4. Why are the stepsisters excited?

   A. They are living in a castle.
   B. They are going on a vacation.
   C. They are going to meet the Prince.
   D. They are getting married.

CCSS.ELA-LITERACY.RL.1.3

2. How many step-sisters does Ella have?

   A. 2
   B. 3
   C. 4
   D. 5

CCSS.ELA-LITERACY.RL.1.3

5. How do the stepsisters treat Ella?

   A. They treat her with kindness.
   B. They treat her poorly.
   C. They ignore her.
   D. They are forced to be nice to her.

CCSS.ELA-LITERACY.RL.1.3

3. Where does Ella work in the story?

   A. the garden
   B. the attic
   C. the kitchen
   D. the laundry room

CCSS.ELA-LITERACY.RL.1.1

6. How does Ella feel in the story so far?

   A. proud
   B. nervous
   C. tired
   D. sad

CCSS.ELA-LITERACY.RL.1.3

The Straw, the Coal, and the Bean

A bean and a hot coal met each other on the highroad, and as they were both rolling along in the same direction they soon struck up a friendship.

Presently they were joined by a straw, and the three began talking together. They were all going out in the world to seek their fortunes.

"It is just a bit of luck that I can travel about in this way," said the bean. "If I had not been a stout active fellow I would have been boiled into soup by now. The mistress was about to throw me into the pot with a lot of other beans, but I managed to slip through her fingers and rolled out through the doorway and down the steps without her even noticing I was gone."

"That was a clever trick," said the hot coal. "I, too, am a lively chap. I and my brothers were set to heat a kettle, but I jumped out of the fire, and I was so hot the cook did not dare to touch me. She pushed me out of doors with her foot, and now I am free to go about the world as I choose, and seek my fortune."

The straw sighed. "I was never as active as that," she said. "Always wherever the wind blew me I went. The farmer had picked up a whole armful of straws to make a bed for the cow; but the wind caught me up and carried me off—and here I am."

While they were talking in this way the comrades came to a brook, and this stopped their journey, for they did not know how to get across. The straw could easily have sailed over on the first puff of wind, but that way would not do for the other two.

"Listen!" said the straw. "I am long enough to reach from one side of the stream to the other. I will lay myself across it like a bridge, and then you can both walk on over me without getting wet."

To this plan the other two were glad to agree, so the straw laid herself across the stream.

"You go first," said the bean, for he was a cautious fellow, and wanted to see whether the bridge was safe before he tried it.

The coal, however, was quick and fiery. He ran out on the straw, but half-way over he grew dizzy and had to stop.

"Quick! quick!" cried the straw. "I am burning"; for the coal was still very hot.

"Wait," said the coal, balancing himself. "Just a minute!"

But the straw could not wait even for a minute. The coal had burned through it, and down they both went into the water, the coal hissing as it fell.

That seemed so comical to the bean that it began to laugh. It laughed and laughed; it laughed so hard that at last it split its skin, and that would have been the end of it if a tailor had not chanced to come by just then.

Have you ever notice a line on a bean? Do you think it came from this story?

"Help! Help!" cried the bean.

The tailor looked all about him, and then he saw the bean lying on the ground. He picked it up, and it did not take him long to see what was the matter with it. "This slit can be easily mended," said he, and he whipped out his needle and thread and sewed up the bean in a trice.

Unluckily he had only black thread, and the stitches made a line of black down the side of the bean. And ever since then, if you look, you will see that every bean of that kind has a black line down one side of it.

Exercises

1. Where were the straw, the coal, and the bean?

   A. on the highroad
   B. in the forest
   C. in the pond
   D. on the roof

CCSS.ELA-LITERACY.RL.1.1

2. Where does the bean think he should be?

   A. in a salad
   B. boiled into soup
   C. in the store
   D. right where he is

CCSS.ELA-LITERACY.RL.1.3

3. What does the straw offer to do?

   A. set himself on fire to help them stay warm
   B. make a bridge so they can cross the stream
   C. go look for help
   D. sell himself to make them some money

CCSS.ELA-LITERACY.RL.1.4

4. Where did the coal go?

   A. into the fireplace
   B. into a stocking
   C. into the water
   D. into the tailor's pocket

CCSS.ELA-LITERACY.RL.1.7

5. What happened to the bean?

CCSS.ELA-LITERACY.RL.1.3

6. Who helped the bean in the story and how?

CCSS.ELA-LITERACY.RL.1.2

Notes

WEEK 16

VIDEO
EXPLANATIONS

ARGOPREP.COM

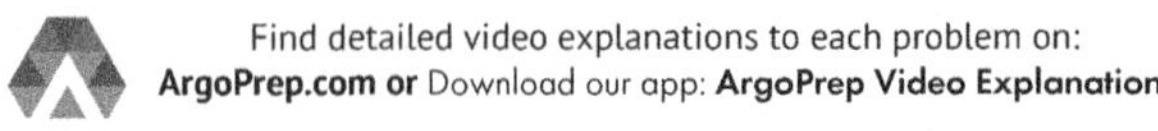

Vowel Teams

CCSS.ELA-LITERACY.L.1.2.D

There are many different spelling patterns that can help you with your reading and writing skills.

Some of the most common patterns use long vowel sounds. Sometimes these patterns involve vowel teams, in which two vowels work together with one another to make a long sound.

Remember: The vowels are a, e, I, o, u and sometimes y.

Here are some examples of **vowel teams:**

ee	**oa**	**ei**
ea	**ai**	**eu**
ou	**ay**	**ui**
oo	**oe**	**uy**

Look at the following sentence.

Which words use vowel teams?

One day, Mary filled her pail with sand while the clouds moved in to bring rain.

The words day, pail, clouds, and rain all use vowel teams.

Vowels can work together to make long vowels sounds. These are known as vowel teams.

Let's practice!

Members of a sports team work together, much like vowel teams.

Exercises

Look at the sentences. Choose the correctly spelled word and write it on the line.

1. Please brush and floss your ________________ before bed.

   (teath / teeth / teith)

   CCSS.ELA-LITERACY.L.1.2.D

2. The red ________________ won the game.

   (team / teem / teme)

   CCSS.ELA-LITERACY.L.1.2.D

3. My mom likes ________________ in her coffee.

   (creme / creem / cream)

   CCSS.ELA-LITERACY.L.1.2.D

4. The ________________ hopped along the path.

   (toad / tode / taod)

   CCSS.ELA-LITERACY.L.1.2.D

5. We will ride on the ________________ during our trip.

   (trane / train / trayn)

   CCSS.ELA-LITERACY.L.1.2.D

6. She had ________________ with jelly.

   (toste / toast / taost)

   CCSS.ELA-LITERACY.L.1.2.D

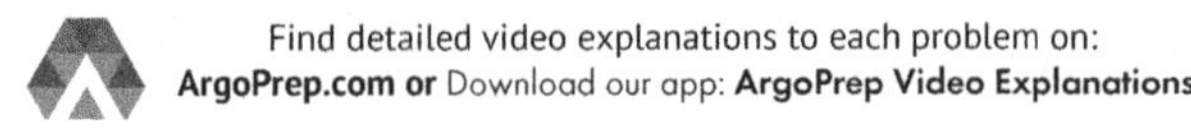

R-Controlled vowels

CCSS.ELA-LITERACY.L.1.2.D

Another spelling pattern that can help you with your reading and writing skills uses the letter r.

The letter r can be combined with the vowels a, e, I, o, and u to make a new sound. When an r is paired with a vowel, the r makes the strong sound. It *controls* the sound.

These vowels work with the letter r within words like this:

ar	**er**	**ir**
or	**ur**	

Look at the following sentence.

Find the words that use a vowel r team.

Her mom drove the car to the store to buy bird food.

The words Her, car, store, and bird all use a vowel and r pair.

Vowels can work together with the consonant r to make new sounds. These are known as r controlled vowels.

Let's practice!

R-controlled vowels all have the same general sound in common.

Exercises

Look at the sentences. Choose the correctly spelled word and write it on the line.

1. We ate yellow ______________ for dinner.

(corn / curn / cern)

CCSS.ELA-LITERACY.L.1.2.D

2. That green ______________ moves slowly.

(tortle / tirtle / turtle)

CCSS.ELA-LITERACY.L.1.2.D

3. The ______________ had pink petals and big leaves.

(flowir / flowur / flower)

CCSS.ELA-LITERACY.L.1.2.D

4. He rode the ______________ around the pasture.

(hirse / horse / hurse)

CCSS.ELA-LITERACY.L.1.2.D

5. That ______________ did a great job in the show.

(gurl / girl / gerl)

CCSS.ELA-LITERACY.L.1.2.D

6. The ______________ flapped its wings.

(berd / bird / burd)

CCSS.ELA-LITERACY.L.1.2.D

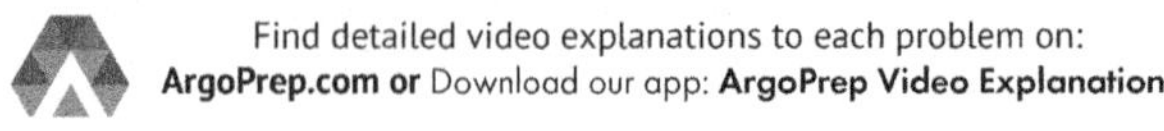

Consonant Blends

CCSS.ELA-LITERACY.L.1.2.D

Some spelling patterns use blends. **Blends make new sounds in words when two or more consonants are placed next to one another.**

These consonant teams work together with one another to make words.

Remember: The consonants are all of the letters in the alphabet except for the vowels: a, e, I, o, u and sometimes y.

Here are some examples of **consonant blends**:

fr	**sh**	**tr**
pl	**sp**	**st**
sk	**gl**	**br**

Look at the following sentence.

Which words use consonant blends?

Brad drew with his crayon on the blanket by the steps.

The words Brad, drew, crayon, blanket, and steps all use consonant blends.

Consonants can work together to make new sounds. These are known as consonant blends.

Let's practice!

Consonant blends can also include more than two letters together like in the word strength. The str- all work together.

Exercises

Look at the sentences. Fill in the missing blends.

1. My favorite fruit is green __apes.

CCSS.ELA-LITERACY.L.1.2.D

2. Don't forget to wear your winter __oves.

CCSS.ELA-LITERACY.L.1.2.D

3. The pretty __owers in the vase were yellow and red.

CCSS.ELA-LITERACY.L.1.2.D

4. The American __ag flew in the air.

CCSS.ELA-LITERACY.L.1.2.D

5. My dad drives a blue __uck.

CCSS.ELA-LITERACY.L.1.2.D

6. What time does it say on the __ock?

CCSS.ELA-LITERACY.L.1.2.D

WEEK 17

VIDEO
EXPLANATIONS

ARGOPREP.COM

Writing a Book

"Let us write a book," they said; "but what shall it be about?"

"A fairy story," said the elder sister.

"A book about kings and queens," said the other.

"Oh, no," said the brother, "let's write about animals."

"We will write about them all," they cried together. So they put the paper, and pens, and ink ready. The elder sister took up a fairy story and looked at it, and put it down again.

"I have never known any fairies," she said, "except in books; but, of course, it would not do to put one book inside another – anyone could do that."

"I shall not begin today," the little one said, "for I must know a few kings and queens before I write about them, or I may say something foolish."

"I shall write about the pig, and the pony, and the white rabbit," said the brother, "but first I must think a bit. It would never do to write a book without thinking."

Then the elder sister took up the fairy story again, to see how many things were left out, for those, she thought, would do to go into her book. The little one said to herself, "Really, it is no good thinking about kings and queens until I have known some, so I must wait;" and while the brother was considering about the pig, and the pony, and the white rabbit, he fell asleep.

So the book is not written yet, but when it is we shall know a great deal.

The ending leaves some room for the reader to think about what the books mentioned in the story might be about. This is a strategy that many authors use.

Exercises

1. What are the children unsure of?

   A. where their mother is
   B. what time it is
   C. what to write about
   D. how to get home

CCSS.ELA-LITERACY.RL.1.1

2. What is the eldest sister planning to write?

   A. an essay about holidays
   B. a book about fairies
   C. a journal about her trip
   D. a story about animals

CCSS.ELA-LITERACY.RL.1.3

3. What is the author's purpose for writing the story?

   A. To entertain
   B. To convince you to do something
   C. To teach you how to write a book
   D. To help you plan out your ideas

CCSS.ELA-LITERACY.RL.1.3

4. What does the brother want to write about?

   A. trains
   B. animals
   C. his family
   D. school

CCSS.ELA-LITERACY.RL.1.3

5. What happens to the brother at the end of the story?

   A. He writes a book.
   B. He goes back home.
   C. He falls asleep.
   D. He eats dinner.

CCSS.ELA-LITERACY.RL.1.4

6. What word describes the children in the story?

   A. angry
   B. indecisive
   C. proud
   D. tired

CCSS.ELA-LITERACY.RL.1.4

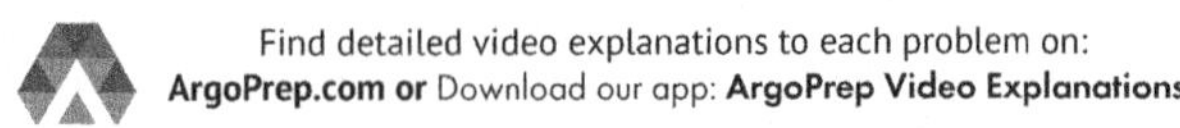

The Sandy Cat

The sandy cat sat by the kitchen fire. Yesterday it had had no supper; this morning everyone had forgotten it. All night it had caught no mice; all day as yet it had tasted no milk. A little grey mouse, a saucer full of milk, a few fish or chicken bones, would have satisfied it; but no grey mouse, with its soft stringy tail behind it, ran across the floor; no milk was near, no chicken bones, no fish, no anything.

The serving-maid had been washing clothes, and was hanging them out to dry. The children had loitered on their way to school, and were wondering what the master would say to them. The father had gone to the fair to help a neighbor to choose a horse. The mother sat making a patchwork quilt. No one thought of the sandy cat; it sat by the fire alone and hungry.

At last the clothes were all a-drying, the children had been scolded, and sat learning a lesson for the morrow. The father came from the fair, and the patchwork quilt was put away. The serving-maid put on a white apron with a frill, and a clean cap, then taking the sandy cat in her arms, said, "...Shall we go into the garden?" So they went and walked up and down, up and down the pathway, till at last they stopped before a rose tree; the serving-maid held up the cat to smell the roses, but with one long bound it leaped from her arms and away – away – away.

Whither?

Ah, dear children, I cannot tell, for I was not there to see; but if ever you are a sandy cat you will know that it is a terrible thing to be asked to smell roses when you are longing for a saucer full of milk and a grey mouse with a soft stringy tail.

A narrator in a story is the person that is telling the story. Who is the narrator in this story?

Exercises

1. What is wrong with the cat at the beginning of the story?

   A. It is lost.
   B. It is hungry.
   C. It is sick.
   D. It is being chased by a dog.

   CCSS.ELA-LITERACY.RL.1.3

2. Where is the cat?

   A. on the porch
   B. in the shed
   C. by the fireplace
   D. in the woods

   CCSS.ELA-LITERACY.RL.1.3

3. Where was the father?

   A. at the post office
   B. at the store
   C. at the fair
   D. at the park

   CCSS.ELA-LITERACY.RL.1.1

4. Which of the following is a synonym for the word *loitered*?

   A. stalled
   B. cried
   C. whined
   D. hurried

   CCSS.ELA-LITERACY.RL.1.3

5. Where does the serving-maid take the cat?

   A. to the garden
   B. to the vet
   C. to the woods
   D. to the store

   CCSS.ELA-LITERACY.RL.1.3

6. What did the cat do?

   A. Ate dinner
   B. Smelled the roses
   C. Purred happily
   D. Ran away

   CCSS.ELA-LITERACY.RL.1.1

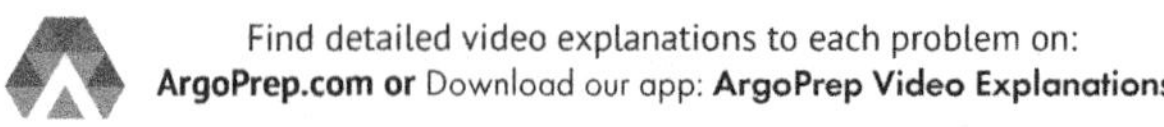

The Proud Boy

There was once a very proud boy. He always walked through the village with his eyes turned down and his hands in his pockets. The boys used to stare at him, and say nothing; and when he was out of sight, they breathed freely. So the proud boy was lonely, and would have had no friends out of doors if it had not been for two stray dogs, the green trees, and a flock of geese upon the common.

One day, just by the weaver's cottage, he met the tailor's son. Now the tailor's son made more noise than any other boy in the village, and when he had done anything wrong he stuck to it, and said he didn't care; so the neighbors thought that he was very brave, and would do wonders when he came to be a man, and some of them hoped he would be a great traveler, and stay long in distant lands.

When the tailor's son saw the proud boy he danced in front of him, and made faces, and provoked him sorely, until, at last, the proud boy turned round and suddenly boxed the ears of the tailor's son, and threw his hat into the road. The tailor's son was surprised, and, without waiting to pick up his hat, ran away, and sitting down in the carpenter's yard, cried bitterly. After a few minutes, the proud boy came to him and returned him his hat, saying politely –

"There is no dust on it; you deserved to have your ears boxed, but I am sorry I was so rude as to throw your hat on to the road."

"I thought you were proud," said the tailor's son, astonished; "I didn't think you'd say that – I wouldn't."

"Perhaps you are not proud?"

"No, I am not."

"Ah, that makes a difference," said the proud boy, still more politely.

"When you are proud, and have done a foolish thing, you make a point of owning it."

"But it takes a lot of courage," said the tailor's son.

"Oh, dear, no," answered the proud boy, "it only takes a lot of cowardice not to," and then turning his eyes down again, he softly walked away.

The author uses the adjective proud in the title. This helps set the tone for what you will read about the main character in the story.

Exercises

1. Which adjective describes the boy?

   A. tired
   B. lonely
   C. tall
   D. angry

CCSS.ELA-LITERACY.RL.1.1

2. What friends does the boy have?

   A. his siblings
   B. his classmates
   C. none
   D. two stray dogs

CCSS.ELA-LITERACY.RL.1.3

3. Who does the boy meet?

   A. the tailor's son
   B. the merchant's daughter
   C. the peddler's cousin
   D. the doctor's friend

CCSS.ELA-LITERACY.RL.1.4

4. What did the proud boy throw?

   A. money
   B. a hat
   C. food
   D. a ball

CCSS.ELA-LITERACY.RL.1.7

5. What happened at the end of the story?

CCSS.ELA-LITERACY.RL.1.3

6. What lesson can you learn from this story?

CCSS.ELA-LITERACY.RL.1.2

WEEK 18

VIDEO
EXPLANATIONS

ARGOPREP.COM

Root Words and Prefixes

CCSS.ELA-LITERACY.L.1.4.B

There are many different parts of words. **The main part of a word is known as the root word. It is the part that most of the meaning comes from.**

Sometimes words have other parts attached to them. These are known as affixes. **A prefix is an affix that comes at the beginning of the word and can change its meaning.**

Here are some examples of **prefixes and their meanings:**

anti-	**against**
co-	**with**
de-	**away**
dis-	**opposite of**
extra-	**beyond**
mid-	**middle**
re-	**again**
therm-	**heat**
trans-	**across**
tri-	**three**
un-	**not**
uni-	**one**

Look at the following sentence.

Which words use prefixes?

Jane rewrote her paper and added an extraordinary ending about a unicycle.

The words rewrote, extraordinary, and unicycle all use prefixes.

rewrote = wrote again

extraordinary = beyond ordinary

unicycle = bike with one wheel

Prefixes work with root words to change the meaning of a word. They come before the root word.

Let's practice!

The job of a prefix is to adjust the meaning of a word.

Exercises

Look at the words. Circle the prefix. Then write the word's meaning on the line.

1. undone = __________

CCSS.ELA-LITERACY.L.1.4.B

2. remake = __________

CCSS.ELA-LITERACY.L.1.4.B

3. cooperate = __________

CCSS.ELA-LITERACY.L.1.4.B

4. midsection = __________

CCSS.ELA-LITERACY.L.1.4.B

5. disagree = __________

CCSS.ELA-LITERACY.L.1.4.B

6. triangle = __________

CCSS.ELA-LITERACY.L.1.4.B

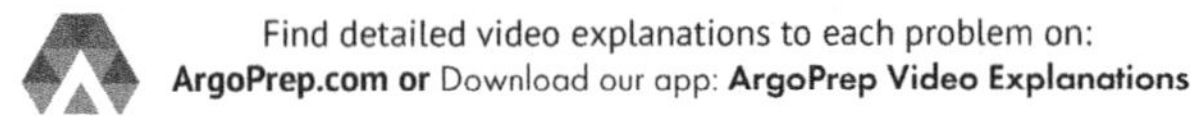

Root Words and Suffixes

CCSS.ELA-LITERACY.L.1.4.B

There are many different parts of words. **The main part of a word is known as the root word. It is the part that most of the meaning comes from.**

Sometimes words have other parts attached to them. These are known as affixes. **A suffix is an affix that comes at the ending of the word and can change its meaning.**

Here are some examples of suffixes and their meanings:

-acy	**quality of**
-dom	**state of being**
-er/-or	**person that does an action**
-ism	**belief**
-ity	**quality of**
-ment	**condition**
-ness	**state of being**
-ship	**position held**

Look at the following sentence.

Which words use suffixes?

An argument almost ended their friendship.

The words argument and friendship use suffixes.

argument = condition of arguing

friendship = position of being friends

Suffixes work with root words to change the meaning of a word. They come after the root word.

Let's practice!

By learning the meanings of many suffixes, you can easily understand new words when you see them.

Exercises

Look at the words. Circle the suffix. Then write the word's meaning on the line.

1. freedom = __________

CCSS.ELA-LITERACY.L.1.4.B

2. leadership = __________

CCSS.ELA-LITERACY.L.1.4.B

3. accuracy = __________

CCSS.ELA-LITERACY.L.1.4.B

4. reader = __________

CCSS.ELA-LITERACY.L.1.4.B

5. sickness = __________

CCSS.ELA-LITERACY.L.1.4.B

6. enchantment = __________

CCSS.ELA-LITERACY.L.1.4.B

Root Words, Prefixes, and Suffixes

CCSS.ELA-LITERACY.L.1.4.B

Let's Review!

There are many different parts of words.

1. **The main part of a word is known as the root word. It is the part that most of the meaning comes from.**

Sometimes words have other parts attached to them. These are known as affixes.

2. **A prefix is an affix that comes at the beginning of the word and can change its meaning.**

3. **A suffix is an affix that comes at the ending of the word and can change its meaning.**

Prefixes, root words, and suffixes can all be combined together to make new words.

Here are some examples of **words that use all three parts together:**

disrespectful

unbelievable

invaluable

undoubtedly

irreversible

illogically

uninteresting

Each of the examples can be broken down to determine its meaning.

Prefixes work with root words to change the meaning of a word. They come before the root word. Suffixes work with root words to change the meaning of a word. They come after the root word. Prefixes, root words, and suffixes can all be combined together to make new words.

Let's practice!

Breaking down words into these three parts can be very helpful as you read. Take off the prefix or suffix and think about how the meaning changes.

Exercises

Look at the sentences. Identify the words that have affixes. Underline the prefix and double underline the suffix in each.

1. She had an unforgettable night at the school dance.

CCSS.ELA-LITERACY.L.1.4.B

2. We will redesign the tricycle's wheels.

CCSS.ELA-LITERACY.L.1.4.B

3. The unicorn drawing was returned to the teacher.

CCSS.ELA-LITERACY.L.1.4.B

4. My remark was in regards to the freedom essay.

CCSS.ELA-LITERACY.L.1.4.B

5. Her argument did not prove to be true.

CCSS.ELA-LITERACY.L.1.4.B

6. She reattached the bow to the present.

CCSS.ELA-LITERACY.L.1.4.B

WEEK 19

VIDEO
EXPLANATIONS

ARGOPREP.COM

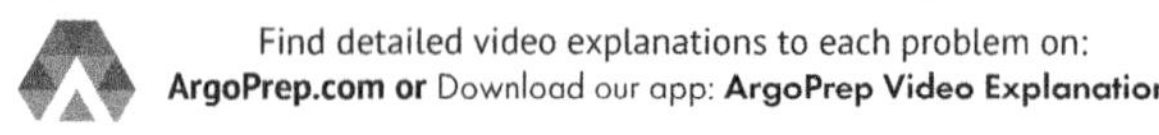

The Pink Parasol

The pink parasol had tender whalebone ribs and a slender stick of cherry-wood. It lived with the willful child in the white house, just beyond the third milestone. All about the trees were green, and the flowers grew tall; in the pond behind the willows the ducks swam round and round and dipped their heads beneath the water.

Every bird and bee, every leaf and flower, loved the child and the pink parasol as they wandered in the garden together, listening to the birds and seeking the shady spots to rest in, or walking up and down the long trim pathway in the sunshine. Yet the child tired of it all, and before summer was over, was always standing by the gate, watching the straight white road that stretched across the plain.

"If I might but see the city, with the busy streets and the eager crowds," he was always saying to himself.

Then all that lived in the garden knew that the child would not be with them long. At last the day came when he flung down the pink parasol, and, without even one last look at the garden, ran out at the gate.

The flowers died, and the swallows journeyed south; the trees stretched higher and higher, to see the child come back across the plain, but he never came. "Ah, dear child!" they sighed many a time, "why are you staying? And are your eyes as blue as ever; or have the sad tears dimmed them? And is your hair golden still? And your voice, is it like the singing of the birds? And your heart – oh! My dear, my dear, what is in your heart now, that once was so full of summer and the sun?"

The pink parasol lay on the pathway, where the child left it, spoilt by the rain, and splashed by the gravel, faded and forgotten. At last, a gipsy lad, with dark eyes, a freckled face, and little gold rings in his ears, came by; he picked up the pink parasol, hid it under his coat, and carried it to the gipsy tent. There it stayed till one day the cherry-wood stick was broken into three pieces, and the pink parasol was put on the fire to make the water boil for the gipsy's tea.

Short stories can give a lot of information to a reader. In what ways does the author do this in the story above?

Exercises

1. Which word is a synonym for the word *parasol*?

   A. blanket
   B. umbrella
   C. raincoat
   D. galoshes

CCSS.ELA-LITERACY.RL.1.4

2. Where does the child wander?

   A. in the garden
   B. near the brook
   C. under the shaded trees
   D. by the railroad tracks

CCSS.ELA-LITERACY.RL.1.3

3. Which word means the same as *willful*?

   A. loud
   B. arrogant
   C. stubborn
   D. old

CCSS.ELA-LITERACY.RL.1.4

4. What happened to the child?

   A. The child got hurt.
   B. The child ran away.
   C. The child took a trip.
   D. The child fell ill.

CCSS.ELA-LITERACY.RL.1.3

5. Where was the parasol left?

   A. in the house
   B. on the pathway
   C. near the water
   D. on the porch

CCSS.ELA-LITERACY.RL.1.1

6. What was the parasol used for at the end of the story?

   A. firewood
   B. a gift
   C. staying dry
   D. a trade

CCSS.ELA-LITERACY.RL.1.3

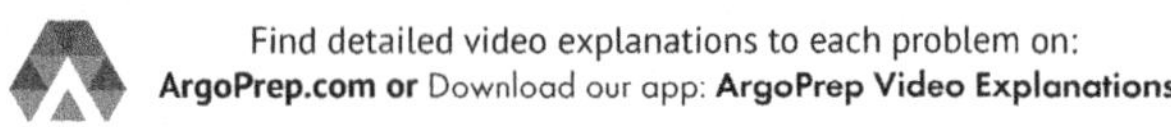

The Swallows

There were some children in the north looking at the swallows flying south. "Why are they going away?" the little one asked.

"The summer is over," the elder sister answered, "and if they stayed here they would be starved and die of cold, and so, when the summer goes, they journey south."

"Our mother and sisters are in the south," the little one said, as they looked after the birds. "Dear little swallows, tell mother that we are watching for her!" But they were already flying over the sea. The chilly winds tried to follow, but the swallows flew so swiftly they were not overtaken; they went on, with the summer always before them.

They were tired many a time; once they stayed to rest upon the French coast, and once, in the Bay of Biscay, they clung to the rigging of a ship all through the night, but in the morning they went on again.

Far away in the south, two English children were looking from the turret window of an old castle.

"Here are the swallows," they said, "perhaps they have come from England. Dear swallows, have you brought us a message?" they asked.

"It was very cold, we had no time for messages; and we must not lose the track of summer," the swallows twittered, and they flew on till they reached the African shore.

"Poor little swallows," said the English children, as they watched the ship come into port that was to take them back to their own land; "they have to chase the summer and the sun, but we do not mind whether it is summer or winter, for if we only keep our hearts warm, the rest does not matter."

"It is very good of the swallows to come to us," the elder sister said, in the next spring, when she heard their first soft twitter beneath the eaves, "for the summer is in many places, and we are so far from the south."

"Yes, it is very good of them to come," the children answered; "dear little swallows, perhaps they love us!"

When reading a text that mentions specific locations like England or Africa, try to find them on a map.

Exercises

1. What season is it in the story?

   A. Winter
   B. Spring
   C. Summer
   D. Fall

   CCSS.ELA-LITERACY.RL.1.3

2. Where are the swallows going?

   A. East
   B. West
   C. North
   D. South

   CCSS.ELA-LITERACY.RL.1.3

3. Where do the swallows rest?

   A. on an airplane
   B. on a train
   C. on a car
   D. on a ship

   CCSS.ELA-LITERACY.RL.1.1

4. Why do the children think the swallows might have brought them?

   A. bird seed
   B. a message
   C. money
   D. cloth

   CCSS.ELA-LITERACY.RL.1.3

5. Why didn't they bring anything to the children?

   A. It was too cold.
   B. They couldn't carry it.
   C. They forgot.
   D. It was too long of a journey.

   CCSS.ELA-LITERACY.RL.1.1

6. What was the final destination for the swallows?

   A. Asia
   B. Africa
   C. Canada
   D. South America

   CCSS.ELA-LITERACY.RL.1.1

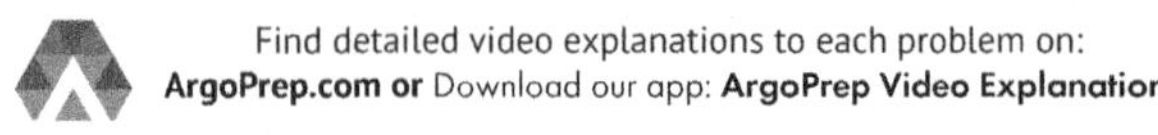

The Kite

It was the most tiresome kite in the world, always wagging its tail, shaking its ears, breaking its string, sitting down on the tops of houses, getting stuck in trees, entangled in hedges, flopping down on ponds, or lying flat on the grass, and refusing to rise higher than a yard from the ground.

I have often sat and thought about that kite, and wondered who its father and mother were. Perhaps they were very poor people, just made of newspaper and little bits of common string knotted together, obliged to fly day and night for a living, and never able to give any time to their children or to bring them up properly. It was pretty, for it had a snow-white face, and pink and white ears; and, with these, no one, let alone a kite, could help being pretty. But though the kite was pretty, it was not good, and it did not prosper; it came to a bad end, oh! a terrible end indeed. It stuck itself on a roof one day, a common red roof with a broken chimney and three tiles missing. It stuck itself there, and it would not move; the children tugged and pulled and coaxed and cried, but still it would not move. At last they fetched a ladder, and had nearly reached it when suddenly the kite started and flew away – right away over the field and over the heath, and over the far far woods, and it never came back again – never – never.

Dear, that is all. But I think sometimes that perhaps beyond the dark pines and the roaring sea the kite is flying still, on and on, farther and farther away, forever and for ever.

This text uses first person point of view. Who might be telling this tale?

Exercises

1. Which adjective describes the kite?

   A. tiresome
   B. delicate
   C. old
   D. shabby

CCSS.ELA-LITERACY.RL.1.1

2. How high does the kite travel?

   A. a foot from the ground
   B. a mile from the ground
   C. an inch from the ground
   D. a yard from the ground

CCSS.ELA-LITERACY.RL.1.3

3. Which colors describe the kite's appearance?

   A. white and blue
   B. red and yellow
   C. yellow and purple
   D. pink and white

CCSS.ELA-LITERACY.RL.1.4

4. Where did the kite finally get stuck?

   A. in an oak tree
   B. on the roof
   C. in an electric wire
   D. on a window shutter

CCSS.ELA-LITERACY.RL.1.7

5. What happened to the kite after the children tried to get it?

CCSS.ELA-LITERACY.RL.1.3

6. Who do you think owned the kite?

CCSS.ELA-LITERACY.RL.1.2

WEEK 20

VIDEO
EXPLANATIONS

ARGOPREP.COM

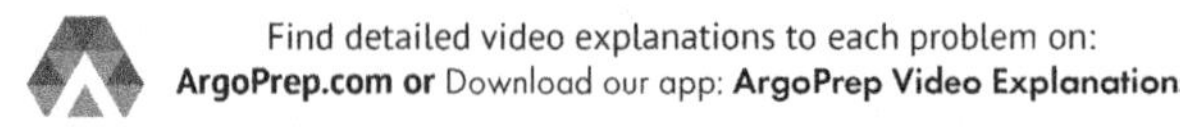

Classifying Objects

CCSS.ELA-LITERACY.L.1.5.A

To classify a word or an object means to sort it according to what it is like.

We can classify words in many ways. Being able to sort them can help you understand their meanings.

Let's focus on sorting these nouns, according to something they have in common.

Let's look at the list below.

boy	**book**	**chair**	**mom**
fish	**rabbit**	**daisy**	**couch**

Now, let's sort them. Some are living things and some are non-living things.

Living Things:	Non-Living Things:
boy	book
mom	chair
fish	couch
rabbit	
daisy	

Sorting words can help you to understand them and how they can be used.

Let's practice!

What other ways can you sort words? How can this be helpful when reading or writing?

Exercises

Look at the food words below. Sort them according to their color.

carrot	banana	broccoli
lime	lettuce	lemon

Green:	**Orange:**	**Yellow:**

CCSS.ELA-LITERACY.L.1.5.A CCSS.ELA-LITERACY.L.1.5.A CCSS.ELA-LITERACY.L.1.5.A

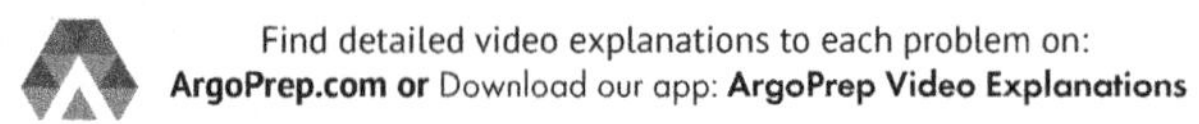

Classifying Parts of Speech

CCSS.ELA-LITERACY.L.1.5.A

To classify a word or an object means to sort it according to what it is like.

We can classify words in many ways, including by determining their part of speech.

Let's focus on sorting these words, according to their part of speech.

Let's look at the list below.

blue	**car**	**cold**	**run**
television	**vase**	**foot**	**soft**

Now, let's sort them. Some are nouns, verbs, and adjectives.

Nouns:	Verbs:	Adjectives:
car	run	cold
foot		blue
vase		soft
television		

Let's practice!

Understanding the basic parts of speech can make you a better reader and writer.

Exercises

Look at the food words below. Sort them according to their part of speech.

friend	silly	hungry
notebook	candy	she
happy	foot	them
child	eat	sing

Nouns:

CCSS.ELA-LITERACY.L.1.5.A

Verbs:

CCSS.ELA-LITERACY.L.1.5.A

Adjectives:

CCSS.ELA-LITERACY.L.1.5.A

Pronouns:

CCSS.ELA-LITERACY.L.1.5.A

Classifying Adjectives

CCSS.ELA-LITERACY.L.1.5.A

To classify a word or an object means to sort it according to what it is like.

We can classify words in many ways, including by their meanings.

Let's focus on sorting these adjectives according to their meanings:

Let's look at the list below.

kind	**friendly**	**rude**	**harsh**
pleasant	**unkind**	**sweet**	**ill-mannered**

Now, let's sort the words by their meaning into two categories:

Nice:	**Mean:**
kind	unkind
pleasant	rude
sweet	harsh
friendly	ill-mannered

Let's practice!

Think of groups of other words that can be classified in the same way, as opposites.

Sort the adjectives by what they can tell us.

smooth	three	shiny	red
tall	soft	five	large
tiny	old	slippery	pink

How It Looks:

CCSS.ELA-LITERACY.L.1.5.A

How Many:

CCSS.ELA-LITERACY.L.1.5.A

How It Feels:

CCSS.ELA-LITERACY.L.1.5.A

What Size:

CCSS.ELA-LITERACY.L.1.5.A

ANSWER
KEY
VIDEO
EXPLANATIONS
ARGOPREP.COM

Find detailed video explanations to each problem on:
ArgoPrep.com or Download our app: **ArgoPrep Video Explanations**

Week 1

Monday
1. C
2. A
3. B
4. B
5. B
6. C

Wednesday
1. A
2. B
3. B
4. B
5. D
6. D

Friday
1. C
2. B
3. C
4. D
5. The grasshopper had enough food for the present time. He did not feel the need to prepare for winter.
6. The moral of the story is to always be prepared. A lesson learned from reading it is to plan ahead for the future. Possible answers may also include: studying for tests, practicing skills to get better, staying organized, etc...

Week 2

Monday
1. B
2. B
3. C
4. ?
5. .
6. !

Wednesday
1. B
2. C
3. A
4. B
5. D
6. B

Friday
1. C
2. D
3. A
4. B
5. Answers will vary, but should include a complete thought that utilizes the word I, begins with a capital letter, and ends with correct punctuation.
6. Answers will vary, but should ask a complete question about the weather, begin with a capital letter, and end with a question mark.

Week 3

Monday
1. C
2. D
3. A
4. B
5. C
6. C

Wednesday
1. B
2. B
3. A
4. A
5. C
6. C

Friday
1. D
2. A
3. A
4. A
5. The children washed dishes, painted sheds, washed cars, planted flowers, mowed the lawn, etc...
6. A lesson learned from reading is that hard work pays off. Possible answers may also include: earning money to buy something, studying hard for a test and getting a good grade, etc...

Week 4

Monday
1. D
2. B
3. A
4. B
5. Answers will vary, but should include a complete thought that utilizes possession with a singular place. For example: I went to Mandy's house.
6. Answers will vary, but should include a complete thought that utilizes the possession of a plural thing. For example: The classrooms' walls were all painted during the summer.

Wednesday
1. C
2. B
3. A
4. C
5. Answers will vary, but should include a complete thought with at least one proper noun (circled) and at least one proper noun (underlined).

6. Answers will vary, but should include a complete thought in the form of a question with at least one proper noun (circled) and at least one proper noun (underlined).

Friday

1. Bill's friends
2. doctor's advice
3. brothers' shirts
4. John's milk
5. baby's blanket
6. cars' tires

Week 5

Monday

1. A
2. B
3. A
4. B
5. B
6. D

Wednesday

1. B
2. A
3. A
4. D
5. C
6. D

Friday

1. D
2. C
3. A
4. A
5. Mr. Brown thinks that Nutkin is rude. He is a bother to him.
6. They brought Mr. Brown three mice in the hopes that he would let them collect nuts from the island.

Week 6

Monday

1. C
2. A
3. D
4. D
5. Answers will vary, but should include a complete thought with a verb that tells what the student does well.
6. Answers will vary, but should include a complete thought with a verb that tells what the student wants to do some day.

Wednesday

1. were (linking)
2. swam (action)
3. goes (linking)
4. sang (action)
5. is (linking)
6. lives (action)

Friday

1. smiled (past)
2. talked (past)
3. run (present)
4. will bring (future)
5. cries (present)
6. draw (present)

Week 7

Monday

1. B
2. B
3. A
4. A
5. D
6. A

Wednesday

1. A
2. B
3. D
4. C
5. A
6. A

Friday

1. D
2. A
3. B
4. A
5. Tom overhears his parents talking about leaving the children in the woods.
6. Tom scatters pebbles along the way into the woods and the children are able to follow them and get back home.

Week 8

Monday

Answers will vary. Possible choices are below.

1. black bear, dark forest
2. happy teacher, blue marker
3. older brother, chapter books
4. delicious food, large family
5. I have long dark hair.
6. The hot sandy beach is my favorite place to visit.

Wednesday

1. blue (descriptive)
2. cool (descriptive)
3. three (quantitative)
4. that (demonstrative)
5. those (demonstrative)
6. two (quantitative)

Friday

1. in, near
2. to, at
3. in, after
4. on, during
5. by, at
6. with, at, on

Week 9

Monday
1. B
2. A
3. A
4. B
5. D
6. C

Wednesday
1. D
2. B
3. A
4. B
5. B
6. B

Friday
1. A
2. B
3. C
4. A
5. A hobgoblin helps the maiden.
6. He is pleased, but he is greedy and wants more gold.

Week 10

Monday
1. She (singular)
2. They (plural)
3. We (plural)
4. him (singular)
5. us (plural)
6. them (plural)

Wednesday
1. I
2. She
3. We
4. it
5. them
6. them

Friday
1. Her
2. Their
3. my
4. our
5. His
6. her

Week 11

Monday
1. B
2. B
3. A
4. C
5. A
6. A

Wednesday
1. A
2. A
3. D
4. B
5. C
6. A

Friday
1. C
2. B
3. A
4. C
5. They saw the word SURPRISE!
6. Alicia's friends and family were there to celebrate with a surprise party. Alicia was happy and Lauren was proud.

Week 12

Monday
1. Melissa and Ben love to shop. (declarative)
2. However you look at it, it will be fun. (Answers will vary)
3. Because I love the hot weather, I enjoy the summer time. (Answers will vary.)
4. Whenever you get here, please take your shoes off. (Answers will vary.)
5. I live in Texas. (declarative)
6. My mother loves it. (declarative)

Wednesday
Answers will vary, but should include a complete thought in the form of a question, and end with a question mark.
1. What day is it?
2. When will you leave for your trip?
3. How can I get to the city?
4. Who will be home tonight?
5. When does she have dance class?
6. Where is your homework?

Friday
Answers will vary, but should include a complete thought in the form of a command, and end with an exclamation mark or a period.
1. Please go to the store today.
2. You need to clean your room!
3. Let's take a trip to Miami!
4. I want you to call me tonight.
5. Put your clothes away now!
6. Stand next to him.

Week 13

Monday
1. C
2. A
3. D
4. B
5. B

6. B

Wednesday

1. B
2. A
3. D
4. C
5. D
6. A

Friday

1. A
2. C
3. D
4. C
5. He searches for a lock that will match the key.
6. Answers will vary and should describe something that might be found inside the chest that the key opens.

Week 14

Monday

1. My favorite colors are orange, yellow, and blue.
2. Remember to pack shirts, socks, and shoes for the trip.
3. I love to draw, color, and write in my notebook.
4. Lunch is after math, science, gym, and English.
5. I have gone to Texas, Florida, New York, and Ohio.
6. My dad, brother, sister, and I will all be there.

Wednesday

1. Before going to see the dentist, brush and floss your teeth.
2. After she got on the airplane, she waved from the window.
3. Upon finding the lost key, Jenny clapped her hands and cheered.
4. While eating her lunch, Aubrie watched the people walking by.
5. Under the sea, there are many types of fish to look at.
6. On Maple Street, Judy and her brother visit their cousins.

Friday

1. July 14, 2017
2. Dear Annabelle,
3. Pittsburgh, Pennsylvania
4. New York City, New York
5. Dearest Rachel,
6. Sincerely,
Robert Denton

Week 15

Monday

1. B
2. A
3. D
4. A
5. B
6. A

Wednesday

1. B
2. A
3. C
4. C
5. B
6. D

Friday

1. A
2. B
3. B
4. C
5. He fell onto the ground, but needs fixed.
6. The tailor mends him with a thread and a needle.

Week 16

Monday

1. teeth
2. team
3. cream
4. toad
5. train
6. toast

Wednesday

1. corn
2. turtle
3. flower
4. horse
5. girl
6. bird

Friday

1. grapes
2. gloves
3. flowers
4. flag
5. truck
6. clock

Week 17

Monday

1. C
2. B
3. A
4. B
5. C
6. B

Wednesday

1. B
2. C
3. C
4. A
5. A
6. D

Friday

1. B
2. D

3. A
4. B
5. The boy apologizes to the tailor's son after he throws his hat.
6. It is best not to be a coward.

Week 18

Monday

1. not done
2. make again
3. operate with
4. middle section
5. to not agree
6. three angles

Wednesday

1. state of being free
2. position held by a leader
3. quality of being accurate
4. person who reads
5. state of being sick
6. condition of being enchanted

Friday

1. unforgettable
2. redesign, tricycle
3. unicorn, return
4. remark, regards, freedom
5. argument
6. reattached

Week 19

Monday

1. B
2. A
3. C
4. B
5. B
6. A

Wednesday

1. C
2. D
3. D
4. B
5. A
6. B

Friday

1. A
2. B
3. D
4. B
5. It flew away and was never seen again.
6. Answers will vary, but should include an owner of the kite.

Week 20

Monday

Green: lime broccoli lettuce
Orange: carrot
Yellow: banana lemon

Wednesday

Nouns: friend notebook child candy foot
Verbs: eat sing
Adjectives: silly happy hungry
Pronouns: she them

Friday

How It Looks: tall red pink old shiny
How Many: three five
How It Feels: smooth soft slippery
What Size: tiny large

Reference

The Project Gutenberg EBook of Aesop's Fables, by Aesop Week 1, Monday
http://www.gutenberg.org/cache/epub/28/pg28.txt

The Project Gutenberg EBook of Aesop's Fables, by Aesop Week 1, Wednesday
http://www.gutenberg.org/cache/epub/28/pg28.txt

The Project Gutenberg EBook of Aesop's Fables, by Aesop Week 1, Friday
http://www.gutenberg.org/cache/epub/28/pg28.txt

Project Gutenberg's A Collection of Beatrix Potter Stories, by Beatrix Potter Week 5, Monday
http://www.gutenberg.org/cache/epub/582/pg582.txt

Project Gutenberg's A Collection of Beatrix Potter Stories, by Beatrix Potter Week 5, Wednesday
http://www.gutenberg.org/cache/epub/582/pg582.txt

Project Gutenberg's A Collection of Beatrix Potter Stories, by Beatrix Potter Week 5, Friday
http://www.gutenberg.org/cache/epub/582/pg582.txt

The Project Gutenberg EBook of Favorite Fairy Tales, by Logan Marshall Week 7, Monday
http://www.gutenberg.org/cache/epub/20748/pg20748.txt

The Project Gutenberg EBook of Favorite Fairy Tales, by Logan Marshall Week 7, Wednesday
http://www.gutenberg.org/cache/epub/20748/pg20748.txt

The Project Gutenberg EBook of Favorite Fairy Tales, by Logan Marshall Week 7, Friday
http://www.gutenberg.org/cache/epub/20748/pg20748.txt

The Project Gutenberg eBook, Children's Hour with Red Riding Hood and Other Stories, Edited by Watty Piper Week 9, Monday
http://www.gutenberg.org/cache/epub/11592/pg11592.txt

The Project Gutenberg EBook of Favorite Fairy Tales, by Logan Marshall Week 9, Wednesday
http://www.gutenberg.org/files/7439/7439-0.txt

The Project Gutenberg EBook of Grimms' Fairy Tales, by The Brothers Grimm Week 9, Friday
http://www.gutenberg.org/files/2591/2591-0.txt

The Project Gutenberg EBook of Mother's Nursery Tales, by Katherine Pyle Week 13, Monday
http://www.gutenberg.org/files/49001/49001-0.txt

The Project Gutenberg EBook of Mother's Nursery Tales, by Katherine Pyle Week 13, Wednesday

http://www.gutenberg.org/files/49001/49001-0.txt

The Project Gutenberg EBook of Mother's Nursery Tales, by Katherine Pyle Week 13, Friday

http://www.gutenberg.org/files/49001/49001-0.txt

The Project Gutenberg EBook of Mother's Nursery Tales, by Katherine Pyle Week 15, Monday

http://www.gutenberg.org/files/49001/49001-0.txt

The Project Gutenberg EBook of Mother's Nursery Tales, by Katherine Pyle Week 15, Wednesday

http://www.gutenberg.org/files/49001/49001-0.txt

The Project Gutenberg EBook of Mother's Nursery Tales, by Katherine Pyle Week 15, Friday

http://www.gutenberg.org/files/49001/49001-0.txt

The Project Gutenberg EBook of Very Short Stories and Verses For Children, by Mrs. W. K. Clifford Week 17, Monday

http://www.gutenberg.org/cache/epub/30272/pg30272.txt

The Project Gutenberg EBook of Very Short Stories and Verses For Children, by Mrs. W. K. Clifford Week 17, Wednesday

http://www.gutenberg.org/cache/epub/30272/pg30272.txt

The Project Gutenberg EBook of Very Short Stories and Verses For Children, by Mrs. W. K. Clifford Week 17, Friday

http://www.gutenberg.org/cache/epub/30272/pg30272.txt

The Project Gutenberg EBook of Very Short Stories and Verses For Children, by Mrs. W. K. Clifford Week 19, Monday

http://www.gutenberg.org/cache/epub/30272/pg30272.txt

The Project Gutenberg EBook of Very Short Stories and Verses For Children, by Mrs. W. K. Clifford Week 19, Wednesday

http://www.gutenberg.org/cache/epub/30272/pg30272.txt

The Project Gutenberg EBook of Very Short Stories and Verses For Children, by Mrs. W. K. Clifford Week 19, Friday

http://www.gutenberg.org/cache/epub/30272/pg30272.txt

Made in the USA
Coppell, TX
19 March 2020

17230900R00105